OLD TESTAMENT GUIDES

General Editor

R.N. Whybray

EXODUS

D1260780

6.00
shelf

EXODUS

W. Johnstone

Published by JSOT Press
for the Society for Old Testament Study

A.T.S. Library
Nyack, NY 10960   22175

לאלישבע
עזר כנגדי

Copyright © 1990 Sheffield Academic Press

Published by JSOT Press
JSOT Press is an imprint of
Sheffield Academic Press Ltd
The University of Sheffield
343 Fulwood Road
Sheffield S10 3BP
England

Printed in Great Britain
by Billing & Sons Ltd
Worcester

#20935425

British Library Cataloguing in Publication Data

Johnstone, W. (William), *1936–*
    Exodus.
    1. Bible. O.T. Exodus. Exodus
    I. Title
    222'.12

    ISSN 0264-6498
    ISBN 1-85075-239-7

CONTENTS

PREFACE

I should like to thank the officers and members of the Society for Old Testament Study for the opportunity to contribute to 'Old Testament Guides', the Press for its patience in waiting for the manuscript and, especially, the general editor of the series for his shrewd advice. The defects of the volume are in no wise attributable to him. Were they not a bit pretentious for nowadays, I should be happy to launch the book with the words of Thomas Arnold: 'If nine-tenths of all that I have said were to be entirely mistaken, I should yet be perfectly satisfied if its tone and manner had invited my readers to think for themselves, and so enabled them to correct my errors'.

Thanks are also due to the University of Aberdeen for granting post-decanal study leave and to the Carnegie Trust for the Universities of Scotland who helped to fund a visit to Sinai.

William Johnstone
King's College
University of Aberdeen
Easter, 1989

ABBREVIATIONS

ANET	J.B. Pritchard, ed., *Ancient Near Eastern Texts relating to the Old Testament*, 3rd edn, Princeton University Press, 1969.
B	The 'Book of the Covenant' (Exod. 20.22-23.33)
BAR	*Biblical Archaeology Review*
BK	Biblischer Kommentar
bPes.	Tractate Pesaḥim in the *Babylonian Talmud*
BZAW	Beiheft zur Zeitschrift für die alttestamentliche Wissenschaft
D	Deuteronomy and matters pertaining to it
Dtr	Matters pertaining to the Deuteronomistic movement
DtrH	The Deuteronomistic History (Deut., Joshua–2 Kings)
E	The E 'source' (using 'Elohim' for God; from Ephraim)
EA	J.A. Knudtzon, *Die El-Amarna-Tafeln*, Leipzig, 1907ff.
EBA	Early Bronze Age (ca. 3000-2000 BC)
EHPR	Etudes d'histoire et de philosophie religieuses, Faculté de théologie protestante, Strasbourg
ET	*Expository Times*
EV(V)	English Version(s)
G	'gemeinsame Grundlage' ('shared basis' underlying J and E)
GK	A.E. Cowley, ed., *Gesenius' Hebrew Grammar as edited and enlarged by the late E. Kautzsch*, 2nd edn, Oxford: Clarendon, 1910.
HPT	M. Noth, *History of Pentateuchal Traditions*
HTR	*Harvard Theological Review*
IA 1	Iron Age 1 (ca. 1200-1000 BC)
ICC	International Critical Commentary

J	The J 'source' (using 'J/Yahweh' for God; from Judah)
JSOT(S)	*Journal for the Study of the Old Testament* (Supplement Series)
KBW	Katholisches Bibelwerk
LBA	Late Bronze Age (ca. 1560-1200 BC)
LOT	S.R. Driver, *Literature of the Old Testament*
LXX	Septuagint
MBA	Middle Bronze Age (ca. 2000-1560 BC)
MT	Masoretic Text
OBO	Orbis biblicus et orientalis
OH	J.E. Carpenter, G. Harford-Battersby, eds., *The Hexateuch. . . arranged in its constituent documents by members of the Society of Historical Theology, Oxford*
P	The Priestly 'source'
VT(S)	*Vetus Testamentum* (Supplement Series)
WMANT	Wissenschaftliche Monographien zum Alten und Neuen Testament
ZAW	*Zeitschrift für die alttestamentliche Wissenschaft*
*	Text not to be attributed uniformly to one source

INTRODUCTION

The books of the Hebrew Bible from Genesis to 2 Kings tell how in the space of a thousand years or more a small family of ancient Semites, the descendants of Israel, grew from humblest beginnings as wandering shepherds on the fringes of the civilizations of the ancient Near East to become a nation, a kingdom and even an empire before tragically succumbing to division, dissolution and the loss of the land which had made their nationhood possible. Exodus, as the second book of that collection, tells part of the story of the early promising years, which even then were shadowed with the threat of disaster.

The book of Exodus falls into clear sections:

1.1–15.21 relates how the twelve sons of Israel and their households, who had been forced by famine to leave Canaan and settle in Egypt, increased in such numbers that the Egyptians began to fear for their own security. They subjected the Israelites to slavery and sought to slaughter all their sons at birth. Remarkably, however, one of these, Moses, was saved alive by the king of Egypt's own daughter and, ironically, was adopted into the royal household. When Moses grew up, he was forced, after impetuously murdering an Egyptian who was maltreating an Israelite, to flee from Egypt to the neighbouring deserts of Midian. There he was commissioned by God to return and lead his people out of slavery. After ten plagues culminating in the death of all the Egyptian first-born, the obdurate Egyptians were finally prevailed upon to let Moses and his people go. But no sooner had they left, than the Egyptians changed their minds and pursued after them as far as the Red Sea. There the Israelites were miraculously saved by the parting of the waters, while the pursuing Egyptians were all drowned.

15.22–18.27 begins the account of Israel's long march through the wilderness towards the land of Canaan, murmuring and rebelling as they went but always miraculously preserved. The story of that march is continued in Numbers 10.11 and is completed only at the beginning of the book of Joshua.

19.1–40.38 is the initial part of the record of events at Mt Sinai, the central section of the whole Pentateuch, which continues down to Num. 10.10. The chapters in Exodus describe the making of a covenant between the Israelites and their God on the basis of the 'Ten Commandments' and the 'Book of the Covenant' (19.1–24.18), the revelation to Moses of the specification of the Tabernacle, where God will dwell in the midst of his people, and of its furnishings and personnel (25.1–31.17), the breaking of the covenant by the people of Israel in the 'golden calf' incident and the re-making of the covenant (31.18–34.35) and the construction of the Tabernacle, on which the glory of God indeed descends (35.1–40.38).

But what kind of a work is Exodus? The answer to the question may appear to be self-evident: it is a history-book. After all, it is couched in the form of a narrative which tells the story of events dated from the beginning of Israel's stay in Egypt to the first day of the second year after their exodus from it.

Exodus, however, is not only a history-book. Interwoven with the thread of the narrative and, in the end, dominating it are stipulations for religious observances, legal practices and cultic institutions. Exodus is thus also in part a calendar and liturgical handbook for religious festivals and in part a law-code.

Even more remarkable, as history books go, is its account of the self-disclosure of God. As in the rest of the Old Testament, the course of Israel's history is interpreted theologically. God's all-pervasive purpose in the life of this people is overtly recognized. The family of seventy are, in fact, children of a promise once pledged by God in covenant to their forefather Abraham; they are the heirs of the further promises of freedom and land. It is God who sees the affliction of those who are thus 'his people'. It is he who commissions his 'servant' Moses to rescue them, equipping him with a wonder-working staff to perform miraculous signs. The escape from Egypt is a miraculous deliverance performed by God. The people thus created by God's initiative and saved by his intervention are formally constituted as his people at his mountain in Sinai by a covenant with himself. The climax of the book is the construction of the Tabernacle, a dwelling-place for God himself in the midst of his people.

The contents of the book thus require the consideration not only of historical but also of institutional and theological questions. Since such disparate materials have all been brought together into one presentation, it is appropriate also to look at the literary formation and formulation of the book: if, as already seems likely, it is a theologian who has finally put the work together, with what purpose did he write, what sources did he use and how did he set about his task? In the light of these discussions it may be possible to come to a clearer appreciation of the kind of work the book of Exodus is.

1

MATTERS HISTORICAL:
CLEARING THE GROUND

EXODUS BEGINS WITH THE STORY of how the enslaved Israelites gained their freedom from their Egyptian oppressors. The narrative format of the story has prompted the seemingly natural assumption that it recounts historical events. Is this assumption correct? If so, how far is it correct?

In order to write history the historian needs primary sources as nearly as possible contemporary with the events to be portrayed. These sources may be official documents, such as annals, monumental inscriptions or decrees, or the often still more revealing occasional or private documents, such as letters, diaries or ledgers. Do such primary sources exist for the writing of the history of this early period of Israel's life?

This chapter will begin with the modern search for sources contemporary with the times of Israel's early encounters with Egypt. It will then outline a number of reconstructions of events, which have been offered on the basis of these sources in combination with biblical material, and indicate areas where problems remain. Finally, in the light of these inquiries, it will raise the question of the nature of the biblical material and ask whether, in fact, historiographical method can by itself do justice to the character and content of this material.

I. **The biblical chronology**

First a word about the Bible's own chronology is necessary. If material inside the Bible is to be correlated with material outside, then it is vital to know the relevant period on which comparable data are to be sought in the world of Israel's environment. The problems besetting the establishing of an 'absolute' chronology for the biblical data (i.e., one which dates the inner-biblical 'relative' chronology by means of cross-reference to datable external events or named persons) are, however, notorious even for periods which stand more fully in the broad daylight of history than does the exodus.

For example, a fixed point for settling the chronology of later Assyrian history is provided by the eclipse of the sun dated to 15 June, 763 BC. The reference to this eclipse in the Assyrian annals enables the dates of the Assyrian kings mentioned in 2 Kings to be established with certainty. But it is extremely difficult to relate the data in 2 Kings on the reigns of the kings of Israel and Judah to this information. The length of time given from the accession of Jehu to the throne of Israel in the mid-ninth century until the fall of Samaria in 721 is some 119 years, according to the Assyrian king-list from Khorsabad. For the same period 2 Kgs 10–18 allows about 143 years for Israel and 165 years for Judah.

If difficulty in correlation is encountered even for periods which are relatively well-documented, from both biblical and extra-biblical sources, it is compounded for the period before the ninth century, from the reign of Solomon back into earliest times, when correlations between the figures named in the Old Testament and historical figures known from contemporary ancient Near Eastern sources cease.

The biblical chronology for the exodus and related episodes thus hangs in the air. It begins from the biblical data, especially 1 Kgs 6.1, 'In the four hundred and eightieth year after the people of Israel came out of the land of Egypt, in the fourth year of Solomon's reign over Israel. . . ' Assuming Solomon's first year to be ca. 960 BC, the exodus must have taken place ca. 1436 BC. If one adds to that the data of Exod. 12.40, 'The time that the people of Israel dwelt in Egypt was four hundred and thirty years', the descent of Jacob and his sons must have been ca. 1866, with Abraham's migration from Haran 215 years earlier (Gen. 12.4; 17.1ff.; 25.26; 47.9), i.e., ca. 2081 BC. The fragility of this chronology is indicated by the fact that in Gen. 15.13 the length of the sojourn in Egypt is reckoned to be not 430 but 400 years, while in Gen. 15.16 it is merely three generations. It is also part of that overall biblical chronology which led Archbishop Ussher in the mid-seventeenth century to date creation to the year 4004. It is possible in any case that '480' in 1 Kgs 6.1 represents the schematic assignment of 40 years to each of the twelve generations assumed to intervene between the exodus and Solomon. If one were to apply the figure of, say, 25 years as the more normal length of a generation, the date of the exodus would be brought down by some 180 years. But even the figure twelve may be schematic.

Further Reading

The most comprehensive collection of relevant extra-biblical sources published in English is J.B. Pritchard, ed., *Ancient Near Eastern Texts relating to the Old Testament*, 3rd edn, Princeton University Press, 1969 (for the Assyrian king-list mentioned above see p. 566 [cf. pp. 280f.]).

Specifically on the question of chronology, see, e.g., J. Finegan, *Handbook of Biblical Chronology*, Oxford University Press, 1967.

There are many *Histories of Israel* (e.g., among those available in English, M. Noth [2nd edn, 1960], J. Bright [3rd edn, 1981], S. Herrmann [1975], H. Jagersma [1982], J.A. Soggin [1984], J.M. Miller & J.H. Hayes [1986]).

A comprehensive attempt to treat the biblical material on the exodus as historical is to be found in R. de Vaux, *The Early History of Israel*, London: Darton, Longman & Todd, 1978.

A useful discussion of approaches and issues is to be found in J.H. Hayes, J.M. Miller, eds., *Israelite and Judaean History*, London: SCM, 1977; see also G.W. Ramsay, *The Quest for the Historical Israel: Reconstructing Israel's Early History*, Atlanta: John Knox, 1981.

II. Ancient Near Eastern sources

Apart from the Bible itself, the historical status of which is the very point at issue, the potential sources of knowledge about ancient Egypt are two-fold: (1) literary, i.e., references in authors whose works have been preserved from antiquity; (2) archaeological, including epigraphical.

1. Until the dawn of Egyptology, the beginnings of which are conventionally dated to the decipherment of the bilingual hieroglyphic-demotic Egyptian/Greek inscription on the Rosetta Stone pioneered by J.F. Champollion in 1822, the only basis outside the Bible itself for reconstructing Israel's relationships with Egypt was surviving ancient literary texts. But these are late, inconsistent and often tendentious. Among the Alexandrian writers, e.g. Manetho (early 3rd century BC, now preserved in Josephus, 1st century AD) assigns Moses to the reigns of Amenophis and his son Ramesses of the XVIIIth and XIXth Dynasties, while Artapanus (2nd century BC, now preserved in Eusebius) assigns him to Chenephres of the Vth

Dynasty, and Lysimachus (2nd–1st centuries BC, also in Josephus) to Bocchoris of the XXIVth. Anti-Jewish feeling is evident in Manetho's account of Moses as a deposed priest of the god Seth, leader of a band of leprous mine-workers in Sinai and ally of the Hyksos invaders from Jerusalem who controlled Egypt for thirteen years. The expulsion of alien leprous Jews recurs in Hecateus of Abdera (about 300 BC), Lysimachus, and Apion (1st century AD). Equally propagandistic are the pro-Jewish accounts in Philo (1st century AD), where Moses is presented as an idealized Hellenistic philosopher-king, or in Josephus himself where the antiquity and nobility of the Jews are portrayed for the benefit of his Roman audience.

Scholars were thus left to guess at the nature and significance of the historical encounter of the Israel of the exodus period with contemporary Egypt. For example, on the basis of Acts 7.22 ('Moses was instructed in all the wisdom of the Egyptians'), the early biblical critic Alexander Geddes could state, citing the Deist John Spencer, 'It is not now a question among the learned, whether a great part of their [the Israelites'] ritual were not derived from that nation [Egypt]' (*Holy Bible* I, 1792, xiii).

2. The new discipline of Egyptology was accordingly enthusiastically encouraged, not least by biblical specialists. The aims of the Egyptian Exploration Fund (later Society), set up in 1882, were soon defined as including 'illustration of the Old Testament narrative, so far as it has to do with Egypt and the Egyptians', in particular, the illumination of the four hundred and thirty year period of Israel's sojourn (Exod. 12.40). Bricks made without straw were shipped at vast expense back home to London irrespective of whether the Israelites had, or could have had, any hand in their manufacture. Since then, Egyptology has properly established itself as an autonomous discipline and the marginal significance of the biblical connection has become manifest: thousands of texts have been recovered, hundreds of sites have been excavated but nowhere in Egypt is there evidence of a specific individual 'Moses' or even of a group identifiable as the 'people of Israel'. The one seemingly unambiguous mention of Israel occurs in a victory stela of the Pharaoh Merneptah, dated to ca. 1230 (*ANET* 376ff.); the reference there, however, is to Israel as a people encountered by the Egyptians in Canaan. As far as their descent, sojourn and exodus as portrayed in the Old Testament are concerned, there can be at most only suggestions of plausible periods and backgrounds.

Further Reading

On 1., a palatable review is to be found in D.J. Silver, *Images of Moses*, New York: Basic Books, 1982, ch. 2.

On 2., see T.G.H. James, ed., *Excavating in Egypt: The Egypt Exploration Society 1882-1982*, London: British Museum Publications, 1982.

III. Evidence for the relations between Semites and Egypt in the second millennium BC

The Old Testament narrative tells how Israel's relations with Egypt in this period passed through three phases, descent, sojourn and exodus. These episodes, though vaguely dated in the biblical chronology, are most likely to have occurred at some time in the second millennium BC and it is, therefore, the Egyptian records of this period which have been combed for evidence of contacts with Israel's forebears. In the event, while no specific evidence has been found in Egyptian sources, it has proved possible to identify parallels to the biblical data. The following are among the most frequently cited.

1. For the *descent* of Semites into Egypt:

(i) the Beni Hasan mural (*ANET* 229, dated about 1890 BC);

(ii) the Hyksos invasion in the Second Intermediate Period (ca. 1720-1570);

(iii) the captive lists of Amenophis II (*ANET* 245ff., third quarter of the 15th century).

2. For the *sojourn* of Semites in Egypt:

(i) a text naming Asiatics employed in a Theban household (*ANET* 553f., mid-18th century), where the Asiatics received Egyptian names as did Joseph (Gen. 41.45);

(ii) a text of Ramesses II from the 13th century mentioning the *'apiru* in building operations (*'apiru* is a term probably related in some way to 'Hebrew', as its Babylonian form *ḫabiru* in, e.g., the Amarna letters, makes more plain) (K. Galling, *Textbuch zur Geschichte Israels*, 2nd edn, Tübingen: Mohr, 1968, 35f.);

(iii) a text of Ramesses IV from the 12th century, mentioning the *'apiru* in the army (ibid.).

3. For the *attainment by Asiatics* like Joseph *to high office*:

(i) the position of Dod as chamberlain at the court of Amenophis

IV in the early 14th century (*EA* 158, 164);
 (ii) the rule by a Syrian between the XIXth and XXth Dynasties
(*ANET* 260, end of the 13th century).

4. For the *exodus* of Semites from Egypt:
 (i) the Tale of Sinuhe (*ANET* 18ff., 20th century);
 (ii) the expulsion of the Hyksos (*ANET* 233f., 16th century);
 (iii) the pursuit of two runaway slaves (*ANET* 259, copy of text
from the end of the 13th century).

What is striking about these parallels is the width of period which
they cover. If they show anything at all, it is that many of the events
described in the Old Testament are entirely typical of relations
between Egypt and their eastern Semitic neighbours, both nomad
and settled, at many times throughout the second millennium BC. If
pressed, they would suggest that Exodus describes specific and, it
must be said, largely commonplace moments within great historical
processes—military invasion, colonization, imperialism, decline of
empire and, particularly important so far as herdsmen are concerned,
transhumance, the annual interchange of pasture-grounds from
desert to Delta and back again (cf., especially, the 'Prophecy of
Nefer-rohu', dating from the 20th century BC [*ANET* 444ff.] and the
'Report of a Frontier Official', copy of text from 13th century BC
[*ANET* 259])—which are far vaster than Israel's relations with
Egypt. Of these complex processes the Exodus narrative, considered
historiographically, provides a drastically over-simplified account
written from Israel's point of view. What the parallels do not prove is
the specific historicity of any of the events recorded in Exodus: none
of them can be identified with an incident referred to there. More
damagingly, if they are true parallels, they actually detract from the
biblical record: the attempt to understand it as historical and to
enhance it by historiographical means destroys its uniqueness and
threatens, rather, to relativize it.

IV. **Some historical reconstructions**

The inconclusiveness of these parallels coupled with the vagueness of
the Exodus narrative about chronology—not to mention the high
incidence of the miraculous within the narrative—should give
forewarning that standard historiographical methods are unlikely to
do full justice to the biblical material. Nonetheless, scholars have

been challenged to relate the biblical record to knowledge of ancient Near Eastern, in particular Egyptian, history and have pursued this aim with enormous, if at times misdirected, energy. Because of the difficulties, however, scholars are divided about even the basic question of 'absolute' chronology. Three broad chronologies can, with variations, be found within scholarly discussion: the 'long', the 'short' and the 'part long, part short'.

1. The 'long' chronology

(i) This chronology starts from the biblical data noted in Chapter 1. I above, which suggest that the exodus must have taken place ca. 1436, the descent of Jacob ca. 1866 and the migration of Abraham ca. 2081 BC. On the assumption that these are indeed chronological data in the strict historiographical sense, search has been made for suitable corroborative evidence in ancient Near Eastern history.

(a) On the side of ancient Near Eastern literary texts, appeal has been made to Josephus' interpretation of Manetho's tradition of the invasion and expulsion of the Hyksos as the descent and exodus of the Israelite 'shepherd-kings'.

(b) On the archaeological side, the references in Babylonian texts at the end of the third millennium to the arrival of the Amorites ('westerners') were felt by many (see Chapter 1.IV.3 below) to be corroborated by the findings of field archaeology that city life had gradually revived inland from the coast after a period of decline at the end of the Early Bronze Age. The migration of Abraham was related to this phenomenon. Details in the patriarchal narratives have been compared with cultural practices evidenced from ANEn. texts of the second millennium: e.g., E.A. Speiser has compared Abraham's passing his wife Sarah off as his sister (Gen. 12.10ff.; 20.1ff.; cf. Isaac and Rebekah in Gen. 26.6ff.) with Hurrian texts from Nuzi. More recently J.J. Bimson has argued that archaeological evidence (especially the destruction levels marking the transition from the Middle to the Late Bronze Ages and the incidence of Bichrome Ware) can be interpreted to support an incursion of Israel into Canaan in the 15th century. Bimson's position has been given wider currency in the 'coffee-table' presentation of Ian Wilson, who himself links the exodus with the ash cloud and tidal wave unleashed by the volcanic eruption of the island of Santorini in the Aegean ca. 1450 BC.

(ii) The problems with such an early chronology (even granting that the biblical data can be appropriately interpreted in a strictly chronological sense) include the following.

(a) In the Old Testament the Hebrew patriarchs are not equated with but distinguished from the Amorites, who are regarded as among the indigenous inhabitants of the land (cf. Gen. 10.16).

(b) The detailed archaeological argumentation for the migration of Abraham in the transitional EBA/MBA period and the arrival of the Israelites in Canaan after an exodus near the beginning of the LBA (the LBA is usually dated ca. 1560-1200 BC), involves a high degree of selectivity and a substantial amount of special pleading in the use of the evidence. Had it not been for the biblical chronology, no archaeologist would have thought of dating the end of MBA later than the mid-16th century, nor the introduction of Bichrome Ware later than the 16th century. Such phenomena are far too widespread in Canaan, Syria and Cyprus to be specifically related to an Israelite incursion, even assuming that to have been marked by armed conflict, and have links with other pottery typologies, especially Cypriote and Helladic, which provide additional chronological controls. The Santorini eruption does not fit the biblical record very well: volcanic ash, however reinterpreted in terms of darkness or as causing skin irritation, does not figure among the plagues in Exodus 7–11; a tidal wave, even assuming it reached the south eastern Mediterranean coast, accords ill with the narrative of the crossing of the Red Sea.

(c) More recent archaeological interpretation by, e.g., M. Kochavi and A. Mazar, links the arrival of the Israelites in Canaan to much later phenomena. Intensive archaeological excavation and surface exploration in the 1970s and '80s find evidence for the coming of the Israelites in the growing number of rural settlements spreading from the region of Gilead into the areas labelled by the Bible 'Manasseh' and 'Ephraim' from the beginning of the Iron Age (IA 1, ca. 1200-1000 BC) with gradual encroachment south into 'Benjamin' and 'Judah'. This, in rather general terms, matches the biblical picture in Numbers 32, Deuteronomy 1–4 and Joshua of Israel settling first in Trans-Jordan in the form of Reuben, Gad and Half-Manasseh before the main drive of the settlement of the remaining tribes on the West Bank.

(d) A disconcerting feature of recent archaeological investigation in the 'wilderness' of Sinai south and south east of the coastal strip has been the absence of evidence of occupation, Israelite or otherwise, from the beginning of MBA to the beginning of IA or even later, at sites plausibly identified as those featuring in the exodus narrative, e.g., Baal-zephon (occupation not resumed till the Persian period, 539-331 BC) and, especially, Kadesh-barnea (no Israelite occupation until the time of Solomon). If Israel's settlement took place from the east, as archaeological evidence and biblical tradition suggest, this absence of evidence occasions little surprise but leaves the wilderness wandering period archaeologically unsupported.

(e) This absence of evidence for the presence of Israel in the wilderness in the LBA has led some, e.g., E. Anati, to affirm a still longer chronology: the wilderness wandering is to be associated with the increasingly copious evidence of occupation dated from the EBA to the beginning of MBA at numerous sites in the Negev and Sinai, including Kadesh-barnea and Baal-zephon themselves. In support of his argument, Anati, like many another scholar, links the problems of dating the exodus and wilderness wandering to those of the immediately following period, the conquest of Canaan under Joshua. Matching the gap in occupation in the Negev, which poses problems for an exodus and wilderness wandering in MBA/LBA, is the gap in occupation from about 2200 until IA 1 at Ai, which, according to Joshua 7f., was destroyed by Joshua and the Israelite invaders. If Ai was destroyed by Joshua, then the conquest, and, therefore, the preceding wilderness wandering and exodus, must be dated towards the end of the EBA. Anati compares also Jericho, where, according to K.M. Kenyon (its excavator in the 1950s), the LBA town ceased to exist by the third quarter of the fourteenth century and thus could not have been destroyed by Joshua in a thirteenth century invasion but only in an earlier one.

The chief difficulty in Anati's theory—even on its own terms—is that, in order to account for the long gap in the biblical record between an exodus and conquest at the end of third millennium and the subsequent history of Israel, he has to assume that 'an entire period' (more like a thousand years!) has been omitted.

(f) If Israel settled in Canaan or even 'conquered' Canaan in the LBA, it would have encountered the Egyptian imperial power there. But of such an imperial presence there is no evidence in the account of the settlement in Joshua or of the post-settlement period in Judges. The more recent archaeological picture of Israel's settlement in the period after 1200 (cf. (c) above) fits the historical evidence for the social, political and military conditions of the time. A fifteenth century date also leaves too large a gap between settlement and monarchy to be filled by the material in Judges. The conditions which made it possible for Israel to settle (the progressive impoverishment of Canaan by centuries of Egyptian exploitation and the incursions of the Sea Peoples from the west) only developed with the decline of the Egyptian empire in Syria and Canaan at the end of the LBA (cf. e.g. the division of Syria and Canaan between the Egyptians under Ramesses II and the Hittites after the battle of Qadesh ca. 1296; the Syrian interregnum between the XIXth and XXth Dynasties ca. 1200 and the engagement of Ramesses III against the Sea Peoples ca. 1188 [*ANET* 255ff.]).

(g) A general point may be added. In the discussion of archaeological data as such from the ancient Near East from EBA to LBA, terms like 'the patriarchal period' or 'the period of the exodus' are inappropriate: these impose on the vast range of evidence for the peoples of the ancient Near East, of whom the patriarchs and early Israel were at most a fringe group, a biblical pattern that is of highly marginal relevance. Even the term 'biblical archaeology', widely current (e.g., in the 'Albright school'), if it leads to such misapplication, is better avoided. Near eastern archaeology is an autonomous cluster of disciplines which have to evolve their own patterns of interpretation of all the evidence, appropriately including, but not dominated by, the biblical.

2. *The 'short' chronology*

(i) The criticism of the 'long' chronology has already provided part of the case for the 'short'. Because conditions in the Egyptian empire in Canaan at the end of LBA were apparently more advantageous for Israel's conquest, most scholars in recent times, e.g., H.H. Rowley, have dated the exodus in the thirteenth century. The stele of Merneptah (cf. Chapter 1.II, above) mentioned Israel as already one of the peoples subjugated in Canaan; it is assumed, therefore, that the exodus must have taken place some time during the reign of Merneptah's father, Ramesses II (1304-1237). If Ramesses II is the Pharaoh of the exodus, then his father Seti I (1318-1304) must be the Pharaoh of the oppression and of Moses' flight to Midian. That it is this, the XIXth Dynasty, called 'Ramesside' after its founder Ramesses I (1320-1318), which is responsible for the oppression, seems to be confirmed by the name of one of the store-cities, Raamses, where the Israelites were employed as slave labourers (Exod. 1.11). If oppression and exodus are thus to be dated to the XIXth Dynasty, the descent must have taken place earlier. The suggestion is made that the 'heretic' king of the XVIIIth Dynasty, Amenophis IV/Akhenaten (1379-1362), who espoused the 'monotheistic' cult of the Aten, the solar disc, would have welcomed the monotheistic

Joseph as his secretary of state (cf. the Joseph cycle, Genesis 37; 39–50). This kind of scenario has been associated by S. Herrmann with migrations of the Aramaeans, to whom, according to biblical tradition, the Patriarchs are indeed related (e.g., Gen. 11.28; Deut. 26.5).

(ii) At first sight, this identification of the Egyptian context of Israel's descent, sojourn and exodus may seem more probable. Its uncertainty and arbitrariness should not, however, escape notice.

(a) The reference to Raamses in Exod. 1.11 is complicated by the references to the consonantally identical place Rameses (Gen. 47.11; cf. Exod. 12.37; Num. 33.3, 5), where Jacob and his sons were installed at the time of the descent, which ought equally to imply the XIXth Dynasty. If one is forced to plead anachronism in the case of Genesis, why not also in the case of Exodus?

(b) 'The way of the land of the Philistines', the name of the route to Canaan forbidden to the escaping Israelites (Exod. 13.17), is most probably also an anachronism, since the Philistines as one of the 'Sea Peoples', who were part cause and consequence of the collapse of the entire LBA civilization in the eastern Mediterranean, only properly settled post-1200.

(c) Even the place name Raamses, though pointing to the XIXth Dynasty, was known until Ptolemaic times (i.e. post-323 BC) and is, thus, non-specific as regards dating. It is perfectly possible that knowledge of atrocious working conditions for labourers in the grandiose building operations of Ramesses II, to whose reign some half of the surviving monuments of Egypt belong, became as notorious as the plagues of Egypt (already know to the Hittites, cf. *ANET* 394ff.). Quite detailed knowledge about conditions in Egypt is displayed by Old Testament writers who had not necessarily been there (cf. e.g. Am. 8.8; 9.5; Isa. 19; Jer. 46; Ezek. 29ff.).

(d) The sole historical point of reference is the Merneptah stele, but how much does it in fact prove? It provides a chance piece of information about a situation that may have long endured: that roving bands of marauding *ḥabiru*, among whom Israelites were indistinguishable, were in the region is already known from, e.g., the Amarna letters of a century and a half earlier. All else is supposition. As already noted, there are several alternative possibilities for the descent, sojourn and exodus of Semites. On the basis of the historical evidence it is more plausible to argue for recurrent processes than for a single event. It may then be better to consider the biblical material in another light and not assume (as, e.g., H.H. Rowley tends to) that its data and the data from ancient Near Eastern archaeology are, so to speak, mathematical digits of the same order which can be added up more or less congenially.

(e) There is no evidence that the wave of Aramaean wanderers reached the Delta of Egypt; the Egyptian records speak rather of the Shosu, the bedouin population of the Sinai peninsula.

3. *The 'part long, part short' chronology*
This chronology associates the patriarchs with the Amorites but also places the exodus in the thirteenth century. It reflects something of an international and inter-faith 'consensus' reached in the 1960s and held in a variety of forms by, e.g., W.F. Albright, K.M. Kenyon and B. Mazar, and has been eloquently advocated by, e.g., J. Bright and R. de Vaux in their respective *Histories of Israel*. The approach, however, merely combines the difficulties and uncertainties of both the 'longer' and 'shorter' chronologies.

Further Reading

The literature on the archaeological and historical matters dealt with in Chapter 1.IV is vast. The following provides bibliographical information on works of some of the scholars referred to above in order of citation.

E.A. Speiser, *Genesis*, Anchor Bible 1, New York: Doubleday, 1964
J.J. Bimson, *Redating the Exodus and Conquest*, JSOTS 5, Sheffield, 1978.

An interesting controversy has been conducted between Bimson and B. Halpern (the latter championing a 'short' chronology for the exodus) in the *Biblical Archaeology Review*, 13, 1987. *BAR* in general, with its lively format and lavish illustrations, provides highly accessible information on questions concerning current archaeological research and the Bible; earlier vols. (e.g. 1981, 1982) contain further articles on the exodus. The *Biblical Archaeologist* provides a similar service at, generally, a rather more technical level.

I. Wilson, *The Exodus Enigma*, London: Weidenfeld & Nicolson, 1985.
T.L. Thompson, *The Historicity of the Patriarchal Narratives*, BZAW 133, 1974.

A conservative response to Thompson has been edited by A.R. Millard & D.J. Wiseman, *Essays on the Patriarchal Narratives*, Leicester: IVP, 1980.

M. Kochavi, A. Mazar, 'The Israelite Settlement in Canaan in the

Light of Archaeological Excavations', in *Biblical Archaeology Today: Proceedings of the International Congress on Biblical Archaeology, Jerusalem, April 1984*, Jerusalem: Israel Exploration Society, 1985.

E. Oren, 'Ancient military roads between Egypt and Cana'an', *Bulletin of the Anglo-Israel Archaeological Society*, 1982, 20-24.

R. Cohen, *Kadesh-barnea: A Fortress from the Time of the Judaean Kingdom*, Jerusalem: The Israel Museum, 1983.

E. Anati, *Har Karkom: The Mountain of God*, New York: Rizzoli, 1986.

H.H. Rowley, *From Joseph to Joshua*, London: The British Academy, 1950.

S. Herrmann, *Israel in Egypt*, Studies in Biblical Theology, London: SCM, 1973.

V. Other problems encountered by the historical approach

When the material in Exodus is treated as though it were a historical source, two further major problems, besides that of dating the exodus, are encountered: the numbers involved and the location. These problems are typically solved by rationalization: scaling down of the numbers; localization of the event. But the presence of these embarrassments should merely confirm the nature of the biblical material as not primarily historiographical, and underline the need for an appropriate method of interpretation. If the true nature of the material is appreciated, such embarrassments are needless.

1. *The numbers involved in the exodus*

Exod. 12.37 gives the number of Israelites involved in the exodus as 'about six hundred thousand men on foot, besides women and children'. On the assumption that most of these adult males were married with families, the total must have been some two or three million. As if that were not enough, the text adds, 'A mixed multitude also went up with them, and very many cattle, both flocks and herds'. Commentators have felt compelled to concede that numbers of this magnitude could not possibly have crossed any ordinary stretch of water by a—presumably—narrow path in the space of one night. Equally impossible to envisage is how for forty years a host of such a size could have been sustained with food and water and its flocks and herds provided with pasture in the inhospitable deserts of Sinai. Modern census figures suggest a total of ca. 40,000 Bedouin in the whole Sinai peninsula. In AD 1882 the figure was as low as 4,179.

Some means of reducing the biblical number has been sought. One way is to assume that the word for 'thousand' (*'elep*) means here 'family', as apparently in Judg. 6.15; 1 Sam. 10.19. But, if so, why would the women and children be mentioned in addition? In any case, that 600,000 is intended by the biblical writer as a genuine number is confirmed by the census lists in Numbers 1-4. It is, therefore, assumed that the number must be a mere exaggeration, as frequently occurs in other statistics in the Old Testament (cf. e.g. 1 Chron. 19.18 where 7,000 is read for the 700 of the parallel in 2 Sam. 10.18) and in texts from the ancient world. It then becomes a matter for arbitrary speculation how many could have been involved in such a desert trek, e.g. Bimson's 72,000. The suggestion of P. Weimar and E. Zenger that the number might have been as few as 150 is the *reductio ad absurdum* of this approach.

2. *The location of crossing of the Red Sea*

Since so vast a host could not have crossed the 10-30 km. of the Gulf of Suez of the actual Red Sea in one night, alternative locations have been sought. Once again, a modification is proposed for the accepted sense of the Hebrew. The Hebrew expression *'yam suph'* (Exod. 13.18, etc.) has traditionally been rendered 'Red Sea' on the basis of the Greek translation in the Septuagint. But, since *suph* means 'reeds' (as, for example, in Exod. 2.3, 5), the Hebrew, so the argument runs, should be translated 'sea of reeds'. Various suitable expanses of reed beds have then been suggested by various scholars at points roughly along the line of the modern Suez Canal from the Bitter Lakes in the south to Sabkhat al-Bardawil (classical Lake Sirbonis) just below the Mediterranean coast in the north. Quite a plausible case can be made out for the narrow strip of sand which separates Sabkhat al-Bardawil from the Mediterranean: at times no more than a few metres across, it is easy to envisage how a company might pass over it on foot while its pursuers in heavy chariots could get bogged down. There are even classical parallels of troops being trapped in this area (Diodorus, XVI, 46; XX 73f.; cf. Strabo, *Geographica* I, 58). On the other hand, *yam suph* does clearly refer elsewhere in the Old Testament to the Red Sea (unambiguously even to the Gulf of Aqaba, 1 Kgs 9.26) and must be so intended in Exod. 10.19.

3. *Further geographical problems*

(i) *The geography of the sojourn in Egypt*

Only three localities are mentioned. Some biblical passages (Gen. 46.28) imply that 'land of Goshen', where the Israelites were settled (Gen. 45.10ff.), lies between the southern boundary of Judah and the eastern Delta. But this seems to accord ill with other features in the narrative, especially a settled community of some 2-3m. It has, accordingly, been conventional to identify Goshen with the Wadi Tumilat, which runs east to Ismailiya from Zagazig (so e.g. E. Naville, the Egypt Exploration Fund's first excavator). A modern parallel to the sudden departure of nomads settled in this area, when threatened with an oppressive regime, has been popularized by A.H. Sayce (*History of the Hebrews*, 1897, 153).

There is no unanimity on the location of Pithom and Raamses (Exod. 1.11): Pithom is variously identified as Tall al-Maskhutah (Naville), Tall al-Rutabah (A. Gardiner); Raamses as Tall al-Rutabah (W.M.F. Petrie, Naville), Tanis (P. Montet), Qantir (M. Hamza), Tall al-Dab'a (M. Bietak).

(ii) *The location of Sinai*

The location of Sinai, the immediate goal of the escaping Israelites, is as uncertain as their point of departure on the Red Sea. Three main areas have been canvassed among the score or so of proposals that have been offered.

(a) The south of the Sinai peninsula, in the vicinity of St. Catherine's monastery, where granite peaks of impressive grandeur, rise to a height of more than 2,500m. (Jabal Musa, 'the mountain of Moses', e.g. is 2,285m. high). The name of the Wady Firan ('the water-course of the rats') in the south-west of the peninsula has been thought to retain an echo of the biblical 'Paran'. The objections to this location include the fact that it is based only on a Christian tradition derived from refugees from Egypt fleeing Roman persecution in the 3rd century AD. St. Catherine's itself, so named after the Alexandrian martyr, was fortified in the 6th century by the Byzantine emperor Justinian. Further, it lies within the region of southern Sinai, where, because of the turquoise mines, Egyptian interests were at their keenest and the presence of Egyptian patrols was to be expected.

(b) The region of Kadesh-barnea, in the vicinity of which Israel spent much of the forty years of the wilderness period. The most probable identification for the site is Ayn al-Qudayrat, the most

fertile oasis in N. Sinai, near the intersection of the 'Way of Shur' and
the 'Way of Gaza'; about 10km. to the SE there is the oasis of Ayn
Qudays, which may preserve an echo of the biblical name. Accordingly,
suitable mountains in the vicinity have been sought, e.g. Jabal Hallal
(B. Mazar), Har Karkom (E. Anati). The biblical tradition, that
Horeb (understood in the Bible as a synonym of Sinai; in the modern
tradition as the range of which Sinai is the southern peak) is eleven
days' journey from Kadesh-barnea (Deut. 1.2) is, however, to be
noted.

(c) It is held by, among others, M. Noth, that the description of the
theophany at Sinai in Exod. 19.18 implies volcanic activity. The
nearest volcanic region is in the north-west of the Arabian peninsula
(cf. the traditions linking Moses with the Midianites).

(iii) *The route of the wilderness wandering*
Given the dubiety about the locations of the crossing of the Sea and
of Sinai, the route between the two can hardly be plotted with
certainty. Pihahiroth, Migdol and Baal-zephon (Exod. 14.2) have
Semitic names ('mouth of the channels', 'tower', 'lord of the north')
and probably lay on or near the coast of the Mediterranean to the
east of the Delta. But Israel is then forbidden to traverse the obvious
route along the coast to Canaan. When they turn inland to Succoth
and Etham, then to the wilderness of Shur (Heb. 'the wall'; cf.,
perhaps, the wall 'to crush the Sand-Crossers' in the Tale of Sinuhe,
ANET 19), with the watering-hole of Marah and Elim, and thence to
the wilderness of Sin, with the watering-holes of Massah, Meribah
and Rephidim, before, finally, reaching the wilderness of Sinai, they
follow a route to the south, the north or through the centre of the
Sinai peninsula, according to the views of the interpreter about the
location of Sinai.

Further Reading

P. Weimar, E. Zenger and their school have published widely on Exodus.
Their estimate of the number of participants in the exodus is to be found in
their

Exodus—Geschichten und Geschichte, Stuttgart: KBW, 1975,
114.

For a brief statement of a view rather similar to that given here—but still
essentially linear in its conception—see

R. Giveon, 'Archaeological evidence for the Exodus', *Bulletin of the Anglo-Israel Archaeological Society*, 1983-84, 42-44.

For reviews of the geographical questions, see

G.I. Davies, *The Way of the Wilderness*, Cambridge University Press, 1979.

M. Har-El, *The Sinai Journeys: The Route of the Exodus*, San Diego: Ridgefield, 1983.

As an example of the eccentricities to which the question gives rise, see

K. Salibi, *The Bible Came from Arabia*, London: Cape, 1985.

VI. How far should the Book of Exodus be regarded as a historical work?

This inconclusive outcome of historical research invites a re-examination and clarification of the nature of the biblical record. How far is it appropriate to regard Exodus as a work of historiography, in the conventional sense that its chief purpose is to trace the network of causation between events at a mundane level using as far as possible only primary sources?

Perhaps even to ask this question is to begin to answer it. However much the material in Exodus is related to historical events—and it will be argued below that it *does* relate to events marking fundamental historical change—that relation subserves a still more far-reaching objective: to portray to the people of Israel in terms which describe their origins, yet which also encapsulate their whole continuing life, the truths of their enduring relationship with God. To use Exodus to recreate the past as one historical event or series of events, however laudable the motive, is to overlook the nature of the narrative as a statement of the accumulated and summated significance of all past experience focused on, but not exhausted by, the primal events. The thrust of the biblical materials is not backwards to recover an original, but forwards from an undisputed original, which absorbs recurring experience within itself and imposes pattern on it, towards the ultimate goal to which the relationship with God strives.

Because the whole is couched as a narrative of the past, the elements within it have under the exigencies and impetus of the narration to take on the character, which may or may not be foreign to them, of being past events and be suitably formulated as incidents. The narrative itself is not a sober historiographical analysis and reconstruction, seeking merely to satisfy the antiquarian interest of

the intellect, but an artistic work which seeks also to appeal to the
imagination and win the commitment of readers or hearers of all ages
and abilities. It employs suitable devices of narrative art to capture
and intrigue the audience.

It needs little more than a first run through Exodus to see that
narration has taken over and supplanted historiography, and that
under the impetus of the narrative portrayal of basic truths as events,
there are many features which, as events, are improbable or even
impossible. Only if historiography is given supreme valuation can
this be regarded as unfortunate, and only then is there anything to be
gained by trying to explain away any of these features: it will be the
view taken here that only by giving these features their full value can
the true significance of the material be appreciated. The negative
task of seeing what the narrative is *not*, perhaps most clearly
appreciated where the historical and historiographical are at issue,
should help in that task.

The narrative as a whole is not historiographical. It is unilinear in
form with little development of policy and counterpolicy by the
protagonists. The characters are 'stock': the obdurate Pharaoh; the
impotent advisers; even Moses, after his colourful infancy (since H.
Gressmann, legendary elements are commonly identified here) and
youth, fades as a personality behind the persona of the mediator.

The setting is also non-historiographical. The almost complete
lack of interest in the geography of Egypt has already been noted.
Geographical vagueness is matched by temporal. Three Pharaohs
are mentioned (the one who welcomed Joseph, the one of the time of
Moses' birth, youth and flight from Egypt and the one of Moses'
return to Egypt) but none is identified by name or dynasty. The
biblical chronology is equally obscure. One set of calculations (T.
Nöldeke) places the exodus at 2,666 years after creation, at the 2/3
point of a period of 4,000 years, which may suggest eschatological, if
not apocalyptic, speculations. The whole is set in primal time within
a primal context: it is Israel's 'myth' of national origins but set within
a recognizably real world where the jagged and fragmented complexion
of actual events has been smoothed down to the essential profile.

The surrealist (i.e., the real portrayed in terms beyond the actual)
atmosphere is heightened by the marvellous and the miraculous;
mundane possibilities or impossibilities are ignored. Two midwives
suffice for the fecund wives of the 600,000 Israelite menfolk;
Pharaoh's daughter gives Moses an Egyptian name which she
explains by means of a Hebrew popular etymology; Moses turns all

the water of Egypt into blood, then Pharaoh's magicians prove that they can do the same; in the fifth plague all the cattle of the Egyptians die but are smitten with boils in the sixth, killed by hail in the seventh and their firstborn perish along with all the other firstborn of Egypt in the tenth; from midnight on the night of the tenth plague there is time for news of the catastrophe to reach the Pharaoh from all over the land of Egypt, for Pharaoh to summon Moses and Aaron and for 2-3 million Israelites, including infants and children, to be driven out of the land carrying all their possessions and driving their flocks and herds.

It must be clear that is is wholly inappropriate to apply the canons of historiography to these and other materials in Exodus. Such points are not to be made in a cheap way to deride its content. It is only when the material is allowed to discharge its proper function and not one which is largely foreign to it that it can be respected for what it is. It exploits lore of many kinds, legend, folk-tale, religious and social institution, all set within a broadly historical context, in order to embellish the fundamental affirmation that the LORD alone directs the course of events. The high incidence of miracle (signs, plagues, preservation in the wilderness, theophany at Sinai) is intended to convey that the action takes place not through inner-worldly causality but in accordance with the LORD's direction and intervention.

But what, then, *is* the relationship of the narrative in Exodus to history? It seems to me wholly compatible with the evidence to find that Exodus, within the limits imposed by its narrative form, reflects the general trend of history at the end of the LBA and the beginning of IA—the destruction of Egypt's West Asiatic empire, the confining of Egypt within its eastern borders and the emergence of new nation states in Syria and Canaan. Exodus is the Israelite version of these events. The Exodus narrative is part of Israel's confession of faith and of the vehicle of the continuing affirmation of the enduring significance of that faith. This is an astonishing outcome of events: the armed imperial might, which had dominated and impoverished the area for centuries, has been neutralized in a way far beyond human expectation or agency to achieve. Israel confesses that this is the work of none other than their God: 'This is the LORD's doing and it is marvellous in our eyes'. It is, thus, a fundamental mistake to attempt to explain away the miraculous elements in the narrative or to decode them into a series of mundane, rationally comprehensible events: the function of the miraculous is to portray, in terms of a narrative related to—but not bound by—history and to many other elements, the unsuspected continual presence and the unimagined active power of God in the detail, as well as in the general trend, of events.

In the light of these considerations one can more dispassionately review the historical and geographical problems which typically confront the interpreter (the 'date' of the exodus, its 'location', the numbers in it, and so on). In the narrative of the exodus the Bible epitomizes, in Israelite terms, prevailing conditions of subjugation and escape throughout the Egyptian empire:

1. The contact between the Egyptian imperial might and the Semitic semi-nomads and *habiru*, of whom Israel's forebears were a part, took place in the desert fringes from Syria to Sinai and in the frontier zones of the Canaanite city-states. This centuries-long process is expressed in the dynamics of the narrative as a 'descent' into metropolitan Egypt and a 'sojourn' there.

2. All the forebears of later Israel knew at first hand, whether in metropolitan Egypt or in the Egyptian empire in Canaan, what it meant to confront an imperial power and to be 'enslaved' by that power. It is totally beside the point rationalistically to seek to reduce the number of those participating in the exodus.

3. Building operations under the least favourable conditions conceivable in the searing heat of the plague-ridden Delta in the time of Ramesses II, the last most successfully self-assertive Pharaoh known, whose name lived on in the colossi, temples and towns he constructed, provide the ultimate expression for subjection. But whether any of Israel's forebears were ever in fact slaves in metropolitan Egypt itself is not of prime concern and the Egyptian evidence need not be forced to provide support.

4. The plagues of Egypt and the exploitation of subject peoples in the Asian provinces of the empire were constants of experience known to all. Within the Old Testament, being overtaken by the Egyptian plagues is held up as a recurrent threat—as is, indeed, being subjected once more to Egyptian bondage (e.g. Deut. 28.60-68). As in Second Isaiah, release from bondage in Egypt is a paradigm for release from captivity.

5. The geography of the desert route provides a clear example of ideological use of the data. The line of escape is not the rational direct route into Canaan—or even into the wilderness. This is particularly clear in Exodus 14: there is a provocative 'turning back' (v. 2), motivated not by human considerations of military strategy or

of eluding pursuit, but by the desire to demonstrate definitively by the miracle at the Sea that it is Israel's God who is the sole agent of the deliverance of his people and of the destruction of their enemies (cf. e.g. the 'recognition formula' in vv. 4, 18, 'the Egyptians shall know that I am the LORD', and the believing response of Israel, vv. 30f.).

It is again as futile, therefore, to attempt to locate this theological affirmation in geographical detail as it is to date the exodus to a precise historical moment. There is no reason to deny that by 'Sea' the biblical writer has in mind the Red Sea. The collocation of place-names from the sand-bar north of Sabkhat al-Bardawil and the Red Sea itself is motivated by his wish to make through the well-known physical features of the landscape—influenced, one need not absolutely exclude, by his knowledge of the strategic possibilities of the sand-bar—a statement about the definitive line where Egyptian encroachment is cut off. Rationalistically to replace the 'Red Sea' by the 'reed sea' is entirely beside the point and one hopes that it may be dropped from scholarly discussion. Much more relevant are those interpretations which find in the motif of the Sea a reflection of Israelite polemical appropriation of the ancient Near Eastern cosmic myths of the battle between the creator god and the great deep (cf. Exod. 15.5, 8, 10). Speculation about the most favourable oases where Israel could have found food and water and pasture for their flocks and herds (cattle in the desert!) is equally irrelevant.

6. One may make again the general point about rationalizations about date, numbers, location and so on, that, even accepting the validity of the grounds on which they are based, they carry little conviction. The criterion by which they seek to evaluate the Exodus narrative is the historically possible, or as nearly credible as possible. But, quite apart from the subjectivity of the view about what is historically credible, the more historically credible the exodus becomes the less remarkable it becomes and the more difficult it is to account for the impression which it has left on the traditions of ancient Israel.

In the light of the foregoing discussion, it seems to me appropriate to maintain that the writer of Exodus (what might be meant by 'writer' is the subject of Chapter 3) is concerned to portray religious institutions and beliefs in terms of a narrative which reflects historical realities only in broad outlines and is concerned only in so far as is necessary to present a verisimilitude of conditions of the general period while being quite eclectic in its choice of detail.

Israel's religion is not founded on historical events; rather, Israel's religious writers are using a narrative form of presentation in which history provides the general framework; for the filling in of the detail, historical circumstances are only one source among many. This complex narrative is the medium for expressing a prior religious tradition: the historical events in Exodus are not the source but the vehicle, not the basis but the confirmation, not the proof but the proving-ground.

Further Reading

B.F. Batto, 'Red Sea or Reed Sea?', *BAR* 10/4 1984, 57ff.;
C. Kloos, *Yhwh's Combat with the Sea: A Canaanite Tradition in the Religion of Ancient Israel*, Leiden: Brill, 1986.

VII. The figure of Moses as illustration of the issues

As with the exodus as a whole, so with Moses the question of historicity has bulked large in discussion. Support for the 'essential historicity' of Moses has been sought in the general consideration that Judaism, like Christianity and Islam, needs a founder. As R.H. Charles has put it, 'A great religious and moral revelation is not the work of a moral syndicate, but is due to the inspiration of some great outstanding personality' (*The Decalogue*, lii). The same point often appears in the more popular form, 'If Moses did not exist, he would have to be invented'. His Egyptian name ('Moses' is the Hebraized form of the Egyptian element 'is born' in such names as Thut-mosis, Ra-meses) is added as further proof.

The latter point is not very strong. The name 'Moses' may provide little more than plausible colouring or Hebraic polemic ('[he, i.e. the LORD] draws out'): knowledge of Egyptian personal names in ancient Israel is evidenced by a number of figures in the Old Testament who bear Egyptian names but who, or whose parents, may never have set foot in Egypt (e.g. Eli's son Phinehas, 1 Sam. 1.3). It may be but a further example of general knowledge of matters Egyptian in ancient Israel.

As for the general point, one might well reply, 'Just so!'. In the light of the discussion in Chapter 1.I-VI, the narrative is to be regarded as a confession of faith which presents a broadly generalized and drastically oversimplified picture of historical processes taking place in the ancient Near East in the centuries of transition from

LBA to IA; it is primarily a theological statement cast into the form of a linear narrative which exploits lore of many kinds, historical, folk, institutional, liturgical and legal. As will be suggested in Chapter 2, much of this lore has been secondarily attracted to the exodus and Sinai as the supreme foci of experiences of deliverance and revelation. It is not likely, then, that one individual, even a Moses, can, historically speaking, have been associated with the inception of all of these practices or even with all the historical processes to which they are related in the biblical narrative. But for the sake of coherence and accessibility the biblical narrative focuses them on one figure.

The quest for the historical Moses, however well-intentioned, thus runs counter to the thrust of the biblical source: a preoccupation with the biography of the great man can only distract attention from the purpose of the narrative. One may speculate that, historically, Moses was, like Joshua, Samuel or Ezra, a significant local figure. He may have been associated with the semi-nomads of the northern Negev, who were threatened by the Egyptian power in the region, whether these nomads were 'Israelite' or 'Kenite'. He may even have intermarried with the latter. As a Levite, he may have functioned at some local sanctuary; Kadesh-barnea would be an attractive possibility were it not for the lack of archaeological evidence there before the tenth century (cf. Chapter 1.IV.1(ii) (d)). The brazen serpent Nehushtan (2 Kgs 18.4) associated with him, sounds like a genuinely primitive feature. It is this local figure who has been extended under the impetus of the unilinear narrative into an idealized pan-Israelite leader.

Even such a reconstruction remains perforce speculative and leaves the reader perplexed as to what is ultimately gained thereby. If this is true of attempts to reconstruct the life of Moses on the basis of historiography (whether minimalist, as by e.g. M. Noth [cf. Chapter 3.II], or maximalist as by e.g. E. Auerbach), it is still more the case with accounts based, e.g. on psychoanalysis, as notoriously by Sigmund Freud, or, more recently, on political science by A. Wildavsky. Any validity which such essays possess, as some of their authors indeed recognize, arises not from the recreation of the actual experience of one historical figure but from the perception of a more all-embracing—in fact, fundamentally theological—truth focused on that figure.

The main thrust of the narrative is theological. The LORD is the sole agent of deliverance. It is only in his service that the human

2````

agent receives any, and then only reflected, significance. Moses is the 'diminished hero' (D.J. Silver); the excellency is of God not of man. The point is admirably caught in the *Seder* of the annual celebration of the Passover to this day: Moses plays no role in it.

Further Reading

E. Auerbach, *Moses*, Wayne State University Press, 1975.

A. Wildavsky, *The Nursing Father: Moses as a political leader*, University of Alabama, 1984.

G.W. Coats, *Moses: Heroic Man, Man of God*, JSOTS 57, Sheffield, 1988.

B.M. Bokser, *The Origins of the Seder: The Passover Rite and Early Rabbinic Judaism*, Berkeley: California University Press, 1984.

2

MATTERS INSTITUTIONAL:
THE RELIGIOUS CORE

IN CHAPTER 1 IT HAS BEEN ARGUED that the genre of the book of Exodus is confession of faith expressed in a narrative of origins. This narrative exploits lore from many sources, folk, institutional and legal, and is set within a framework which views from an Israelite perspective—and drastically oversimplifies—the historical conditions of the period of transition from Late Bronze Age to Iron Age 1. The purpose is not to reconstruct the past for its own sake but to express the constants of Israel's experience of life under God. Religious institution, as one of the chief ways of expressing and experiencing life under God, provides congenially one of the mainsprings of this narrative.

There are six main institutions or complexes of institutions articulated in narrative form in Exodus: the Festival of Passover, the Festival of Unleavened Bread, the Offering of Firstlings, Theophany, Covenant and Law. These institutions are some of the most important means whereby Israel lived out its community life under God in the annual cycle of worship and in the daily round of affairs. Through them hope for the future was affirmed in the light of origins over against the often bitter experience of present reality. These actualities of life expressed through shared institutional practice are in Exodus gathered up into a coherent narrative. In mutual interaction, this narrative draws from these institutions and imparts to them definitive interpretation.

In Exodus, these six institutions appear in two groups of three: Passover, Unleavened Bread and Firstlings are dealt with in chapters 12–13 within the wider context of the exodus (chs. 1.1–15.21); Theophany, Covenant and Law in chs. 19–24 within the wider context of revelation at Sinai (Exod. 19.1–Num. 10.10). It will be argued below that in each case, surprisingly enough perhaps at first sight, an institution, which has in origin nothing whatever to do with either exodus or Sinai, is secondarily associated with one or the other ('historicized' is the usual term, but, in the light of Chapter 1, that places too high a premium on 'history' to the exclusion of all else). The purpose of this secondary association is that each institution, which has in all probability been observed from time immemorial and has, thus, imparted to all participants a shared expression of communal life, may receive definitive interpretation and become a fully appropriate vehicle for expressing corporate understanding and identity in terms of Israel's faith.

I. **Passover**

Exod. 12.1–13.16 is both legislation (12.1-27, 43-49; 13.1-16) and account of putting legislation into effect (12.28-42, 50f.). But of the three practices legislated for, Passover, Unleavened Bread and Firstlings, it is only Passover (12.1-13, 21-27, 43-50) that could have been practicable, and then only partially, on the original occasion as envisaged by the narrative—Unleavened Bread (12.14-20; 13.3-10), a seven-day pilgrimage festival held at the sanctuary (Exod. 23.14f.), could not be observed while the Egyptians were in hot pursuit; Firstlings (13.1f., 11-16), offered on the eighth day after birth (Exod. 22.30 [Heb. 29]), depended on the season of birth and are obviously quite different from the yearling lamb/kid chosen for Passover (12.5). Thus, despite the initial impression of uniformity in these chapters, where legislation on Passover-Unleavened Bread-Passover-Firstlings-Unleavened Bread-Firstlings is interwoven, only Passover is relevant to exodus and the other two have been brought secondarily into association with it in order to receive added justification (13.8, 14f.). This secondary association with the exodus of practices which have in origin nothing whatever to do with it, in order to impart additional warrant or significance to them, is not uncommon in the Old Testament: thus, e.g., circumcision (Josh. 5.9), sabbath (Deut. 5.15), the Festival of Tabernacles (Lev. 23.43), the whole sacrificial system (Lev. 22, climaxing in v. 33), the Jubilee (Lev. 25.55) and, even, just weights and measures (Lev. 19.35ff.).

But is even the Passover quite at home in the context of the exodus as portrayed in Exod. 12f.? The historical implausibility of certain features of that account have already been noted in Chapter 1. Nor could the complete range of stipulations concerning the Passover have been kept on the night of the exodus: any part of the Passover lamb left till the following morning was to be burnt (12.10) and no

Israelite was to leave his house until the morning (12.22)—but Moses and Aaron were summoned to audience with Pharaoh that night (12.31) and the people of Israel were hustled out of the land, seemingly forthwith. There is, thus, a certain tension between the legislation on the Passover and the account of its first observance: the narrative is created to provide an aetiology for the Passover but, once launched, has to follow a course dictated by its own momentum.

Is it possible, then, that the Passover also, like Unleavened Bread and Firstlings, was an independent institution, which had in origin nothing to do with the exodus, yet has been secondarily associated with it and, indeed, has provided the decisive mould within which the narrative of the exodus has been cast? Writers on the Passover, e.g., J.B. Segal or J. Henninger, have drawn attention to anthropological parallels among the Bedouin of Sinai or among pre-Islamic Arabs to elements within the exodus narrative: the Bedouin custom of smearing the blood of a slaughtered animal at the entrance to a house threatened with cholera, the flesh being eaten in a common meal called a *fidyah* (cf. Hebrew *padah*, 'redeem', used e.g. in Exod. 13.13, 15). Similar rites are practised on many occasions of new beginnings: the breaking-in of new ground, the opening of a new well, the building of a new house, at betrothal and marriage. The purpose of these rites is apotropaic, i.e. to ward off any malign influence that may lurk to harm the participants. The similarity to the Israelites' daubing the lintel and two doorposts of their houses to ward off 'the destroyer' (Exod. 12.23) is surely striking. Among the Bedouin and the pre-Islamic Arabs there is also evidence of a spring rite of offering a blood-sacrifice of the first-born of the herd, which must be without blemish and, preferably, male, followed by a communion meal often with the sprinkling or arointing with sacrificial blood. The purpose of the rite is again to secure protection for the community, their possessions and their herds in the ensuing year.

These parallels can be linked, following the suggestions by L. Rost, still more dynamically to the biblical material. It is striking that the selection of the Passover lamb/goat falls on the tenth day of the first month inasmuch as it is precisely on the tenth day of the seventh month, the Day of Atonement, that the 'scapegoat' is driven out into the wilderness to Azazel, in Jewish tradition the desert demon. The two halves of the pastoral year of the nomad are thus matched by two corresponding rites: the Passover lamb/goat is slain in the first month around the time of the spring equinox, which marks the seasonal change from the winter months with their modest grazing in the wilderness pastures, to the aridity of summer, when the shepherd is driven with his flocks into the stubble fields of the peasant for meagre forage; correspondingly in the seventh month, around the time of the autumn equinox, when the early rains are expected, allowing agriculture once more to begin and the pastures of the wilderness once again to flourish, the scapegoat is driven off into the wilderness. It is difficult not to see in these institutions the vestige of immemorial nomadic rites aimed at warding off malevolent forces as the shepherd and his troupe set off into the potentially threatening environments of the agricultural lands in the spring and of the desert fringes in the autumn. Passover and Day of Atonement both have roots in the rhythms of transhumance, the seasonal migration of stock in search of grazing, which have belonged to pastoral life since time began.

It may even be that the Exodus narrative reflects this primordial spring rite in Moses' request to Pharaoh for permission to go three days' journey into the wilderness to hold festival to Israel's God (Exod. 3.18, etc.). Moses' request would then not be simply an *ad hoc* device to secure the release of his people but would correspond to age-old custom now about to be invested with revolutionary significance. The practice of transhumance is referred to in Egyptian texts (cf. *ANET* 259, 446 cited in Chapter 1).

It is in the light of such a nomadic pastoral background that details of Passover observance can be appreciated. The victim is selected from the small cattle, the sheep and goats, of a pastoral community. Alone of all the festivals of Israel, the Passover was held at night, the appropriate time after the heat of the day when the flocks had finished their foraging and the shepherds had returned to camp. It had to be finished before daybreak, when the flocks would set out once more to seek pasture, hence the preparedness for the swift departure ('your loins girded, your sandals on your feet, and your staff in your hand', Exod. 12.11). As would befit a nomadic society, the animal was not sacrificed at a sanctuary nor offered by a priest; the head of the family himself was the officiant, roasting the flesh of the victim as on the Bedouin's improvised spit over an open fire on the domestic hearth. The victim was eaten with the unleavened bread of travelling folk and the uncultivated wild herbs of the wilderness.

The original separateness of even Passover from the exodus is, thus, a lively possibility. One circumstance makes this even more likely. If the association of Passover with transhumance is correct, it should have been observed as a spring rite of passage from the desert to the sown. Departure *from* the land of Egypt into the wilderness is exactly the opposite of what is to be expected at this season. There is, however, another passage in the Old Testament where the spring rite of transition from the desert into the sown is observed in consonance with the seasonal realities: the narrative of the entry into the land of Canaan in Josh. 1–6 places the event precisely at the time of Passover (Josh. 5.10) and, furthermore, at the time of the barley harvest (Josh. 3.15), in connection with which the festival of Unleavened Bread was observed at the sanctuary at Gilgal (Josh. 5.11). It may be that it was from the resources of age-old observances such as at Gilgal that some of the ideas, which lie at the base of the exodus narrative, were nurtured in Israel's consciousness. It is equally striking that the narrative of crossing the Jordan in Josh. 3.14ff. contains distinct parallels to the narrative of crossing the Red Sea in Exodus 14. Institutional considerations can thus support the archaeological findings noted above: Israel's forebears belong to the wave of Aramaeans encroaching from north-east Transjordan, whose contact with Egyptian oppression was in the imperial provinces of Canaan, not in the metropolitan Egypt of the Nile valley and Delta.

The argument which seems to be developing is, thus, the following. In the exodus narrative Israel's immemorial religious institutions, in particular the Passover, are secondarily associated with historical processes. On the one hand, they receive new and definitive significance from these processes; on the other, they become the means whereby the continuing significance of these historical processes is expressed and reappropriated by the celebrating community. Israel's institutions in their definitive interpretation are unfolded as story in terms of the realities of experience, using lore of manifold kinds. The Passover (also in its Christian guise of Lord's Supper), as the still continuing annual celebration thus definitively interpreted in terms of God's deliverance of his people from slavery in Egypt, is clearly the most potent single force for expressing and reinforcing identity as a family of the people of God. But the secondariness of the association of Passover, as of Unleavened Bread and Firstlings, with exodus should not be overlooked. It is not inappropriately expressed by the phrase which recurs in the legislation for the observance of each: it is only 'when you come to the land/when the LORD brings you into the land' that 'you shall keep this service/set apart to the LORD. . . ' (Passover, Exod. 12.25; Unleavened Bread, 13.5; Firstlings 13.11).

Further Reading

The standard textbook on Israel's religious institutions is

R. de Vaux, *Ancient Israel: Its Life and Institutions*, London:
    Darton, Longman & Todd, 1961.

As in his *History*, de Vaux presents somewhat more 'conservative' views than those offered here.

J.B. Segal, *Hebrew Passover*, London: School of Oriental and
    African Studies, 1963.

J. Henninger, *Les fêtes de printemps chez les sémites et la pâque
    israélite*, Paris: Gabalda, 1975.

L. Rost, *Das kleine Credo*, Heidelberg: Quelle & Meyer, 1965,
    101ff.

II. Unleavened Bread

The impossibility of observing the seven-day pilgrimage festival of Unleavened Bread on the occasion of the exodus (Exod. 12.14-20; 13.3-10) has been noted in Chapter 2.I and provides a *prima facie* case for the secondariness of associating this festival with it. This secondariness may be confirmed by the clear separateness of Unleavened Bread and Passover in the legislation on the festivals in Exod. 23.14-19 and its parallel in Exod. 34.18-26. While the Passover was a pastoral rite, celebrated by the family in the household, Unleavened Bread, which marks the beginning of the barley harvest, was one of the three annual harvest festivals of a farming community, when all the males went on pilgrimage to the sanctuary (the other two harvest festivals were Weeks, which was held seven weeks after the beginning of barley harvest and marked the end of wheat harvest, and Ingathering/Tabernacles, at the autumn equinox, which celebrated the bringing of the winnowed grain from threshing-floor into granary, and the vintage). While in the present form of the legislation in Exod. 12.14ff. Passover is celebrated on the night of the 14th and Unleavened Bread from the 15th till the 21st, this association may be secondary: the timing of Unleavened Bread may in earlier days have depended on the date of the ripening of the barley, which must have varied from locality to locality and from season to season (cf. Deut. 16.9).

The original separateness of Passover and Unleavened Bread is probable also on sociological grounds: Unleavened Bread, as the festival which marks the inauguration of the harvest season, is clearly a farmers' festival; as argued above, Passover is, by contrast, a shepherds' festival. Passover and Unleavened Bread thus represent the rites observed in the two distinct 'morphemes' of Israelite society, the pastoral and the peasant.

Unleavened Bread has, however, been brought into association with Passover in order to give it normative interpretation. This association is facilitated by the coincidence of two features between the two festivals: both are spring rites; in both unleavened bread is eaten. The need for such a normative interpretation of an indigenous farmers' rite in terms of Israel's faith as expressed in the narrative of an 'exodus from Egypt' is suggested by such an incident as 2 Sam. 21.1-14, where entirely heterodox rites are practised from the beginning of the barley harvest. These heterodox rites are further illumined by the beliefs of the indigenous Canaanite population in the dying of Baal in the ripened and winnowed grain in the drought of summer, and his rising again in the springing grain with the coming of the autumn rains, as expressed in the myths of ancient Ugarit. This normative interpretation of Unleavened Bread is also found in the hortatory additions to the legislation on the festival in Exod. 23.15; 34.18.

Further Reading

For two 'morphemes' in Israelite society, see the works of M.B. Rowton, e.g.

'Dimorphic Structure and the Problem of the *'apiru-'Ibrim'*, *Journal of Near Eastern Studies* 35, 1976, 13ff.

For the Ugaritic texts, see

J.C.L. Gibson, *Canaanite Myths and Legends*, Edinburgh: T. & T. Clark, 2nd edn., 1978, e.g., p. 77.

III. Firstlings

If Passover and, to a more limited extent, Unleavened Bread are thus unfolded as story as part of the narrative of Israel's deliverance from Egypt, how far is this also true of Firstlings? Firstlings and Firstfruits were offered from time immemorial (cf. Gen. 4.3f.). The reason for the offering was, presumably, the self-evident one of rendering tribute to God as the giver of fertility in flock and field; by this token—the offering of the first-born and the firstfruits—the whole progeny and produce were hallowed and, at the same time, the remaining progeny and produce were desacralized and made available for ordinary human purposes (cf. Exod. 22.29f. [Heb. 28f.]; Deut. 26.1-11).

But the first-born son of the human family is to be redeemed. Elsewhere it is the Levites who vicariously bear the cost of the redemption of the Israelite first-born sons (Num. 3.11ff., 40ff.). By contrast, in Exodus 13 the institution of Firstlings and the redemption of Israelite first-born sons (vv. 1f., 11-13) are brought into association with the exodus and thus given secondary justification (vv. 14f.): it was at the cost of the first-born males throughout Egypt, both of man and of beast, that Israel's dedication to the LORD and freedom were purchased. The exodus now provides the aetiology not only for Israel's freedom but for the offering of the Israelite Firstlings, whereby that freedom was symbolized. The freedom once purchased at the cost of the Egyptian first-born is not merely a far-off, once-for-all event; it is not only sacramentally reappropriated once per year by the celebrating family and community in the conjoint festival of Passover-Unleavened Bread; it is reaffirmed throughout the year on the eighth day after the birth of every first-born male, whether of human or of domestic animal, and constantly made present in every family by the continuing presence of the redeemed eldest son.

The whole narrative of the exodus (Exod. 11.1–13.16) is thus contained within the framework of the death of the Egyptian first-born. But, since the death of the Egyptian first-born—as the tenth, climactic, plague—links up with the complete plague cycle beginning in 7.14, the literary impact of the elaboration of Firstlings has been very considerable (many commentators link the tenth plague to Passover rather than Firstlings, hardly correctly). Other motifs, like the hardening of Pharaoh's heart and the despoiling of the Egyptians, confirm the link still more widely back to ch. 3.

It is not unlikely that the elaboration of many of the first nine plagues is dependent again on commonplace general knowledge of conditions in Egypt. It is not difficult to imagine that the first plague, the turning of the waters of the Nile into blood, is a popular version of the annual Nile flood, when the waters are heavy with suspended silt. The unfailing regularity of the phenomemon must have been well known (cf. again Am. 8.8; 9.5; the night of 17th June is still known in Egypt as *laylat al-nuqtah* 'the night of the drop', because it is believed that annually on that night the first drop, which causes the Nile flood, falls from the heavens). The immediately following plagues are then not difficult to understand: the frogs, which swarmed throughout the land from the flood-waters; the gnats and flies which multiplied from their dead bodies; the spread of disease on animal and human. The remaining plagues of hail, locusts and darkness 'that could be felt' (eclipse(?)/sirocco(?)) are equally stereotyped as divine visitations.

The secondary association of Firstlings with the exodus has thus had a dynamic effect on the presentation of the narrative. As the basis for the introduction of the tenth plague, its influence extends back to the motif of the hardening of Pharaoh's heart in ch. 3; in the process it has gathered to itself a wide selection of materials drawn from popular lore.

IV. **Theophany**

Theophany—the self-disclosure of God—must be regarded as the central theme of Exodus. Though God is everywhere and can appear anywhere, yet within Exodus, as generally within the Old Testament as a whole, theophany is not mere sporadic mystical encounter with the numinous—though it can be that—but usually has its institutional counterparts. The fundamental institutional counterpart to theophany is the sanctuary.

It may be helpful to sketch the concept of the sanctuary which appears to have been current in the North-West Semitic world of Israel's origins, for the distinctive features of the Israelite conception of the sanctuary can perhaps best be seen as modifications of that model. The primary element of a sanctuary was the *bamah*, the 'high place', the local counterpart of the cosmic mountain on which the Deity was conceived as dwelling and where he sat enthroned as cosmic king. An essential element of the *bamah* is the altar (the 'horns' of the altar may themselves have been regarded as models of the cosmic mountain), the meeting-place between the physical and the spiritual realms, symbolized by the fire on the altar, which transposed the material sacrifice into the smoke ascending into the heavens. A temple as such is not essential; it is in principle merely a *bet bamah*, a 'house of a high place'. But where a temple is built, it too is regarded as the local counterpart of the cosmic dwelling-place of God, which in its plan and furnishings symbolizes elements of the cosmic realm.

These features and concepts enable one to link together a number of elements in the Exodus narrative. It is naturally at a mountain, seemingly already known as the 'mountain of God', equated with

Sinai/Horeb, that Moses encounters God (Exod. 3.1): the LORD, too, has his mountain, whence he exercises his dominion even over Egypt and, thus, the destinies of nations (this concept is greatly developed in connection with Mount Zion; cf. the 'Enthronement Psalms' 47, 93, 96-99 and the Psalm in Exod. 15, already noted in Chapter 1.VI in connection with the conflict with the Sea). (The fire of the burning bush [Exod. 3.2ff.] is best understood as the symbol, not of theophany as so often in the Bible, e.g. in Exodus itself at 19.18, but of persecution despite which God's people Israel, symbolized by the bush, is not consumed. Here God appears not *as* fire, but *in* the fire.) The mountain where God had appeared to Moses becomes the rendez-vous after the exodus: the place of theophany becomes a sanctuary—where God has appeared once, he may be expected to appear again. It is here that Jethro, priest of Midian, encounters Moses his son-in-law again (Exod. 18). The fact that Jethro takes the lead in the sacrifice at God's altar may suggest that this mountain had already been a Kenite shrine (assuming one can derive such historical data from the chapter); it at least lends confirmation to the view that here Israel was participating in generally recognized rites. The climactic theophany and revelation follow in Exodus 19ff.

Numerous details in Exodus 19ff. are of significance for the Israelite conception of theophany. The description of the theophany is, in part, metaphorical in order to express in the most impressive terms available the awesome grandeur of God's self-manifestation: thus the meteorological imagery of storm-cloud, thunder, lightning, with the appropriate geophysical response of volcanic eruption and earthquake (19.16, 18). But the mythological overtones of the imagery should not be overlooked: in the Ugaritic texts Baal 'rides the clouds' and manifests himself in the thunder and lightning (cf. the stele from Ugarit in The Louvre with Baal brandishing the mace [thunder] in his right hand and the spear with zigzag shaft [lightning] in his left). At Sinai the God of Israel is portrayed with the stock North-West Semitic accoutrements of deity.

In part, however, Exodus uses the institutional symbolism of the temple cult: the descending fire is suggestive of the altar-fire, which in principle descends from God himself (Lev. 9.24; 1 Kgs 18.24). It is this fire which provides the pillar of cloud by day and of fire by night rising from the perpetual burnt-offering on the altar. Rationalistic considerations about the improbability of a perpetually burning transportable altar which guides Israel through the wilderness should not blind one to the source of the imagery: as in the surrealist history and geography of the exodus, so in the religious institutions an ideal theological statement is being made. The altar with its continual burnt offering expresses the universal—and, therefore, omnipresent—reality of the unbroken communion between God and people and is, thus, the appropriate symbol for the presence of God, whether guarding his people from the pursuing Egyptians or guiding them through the wilderness.

There is a further element in the symbolism of the cloud. It is from the altar-fire descending from God himself that the coals are taken for the firepan on which incense is burnt. The incense cloud, kindled from God's own altar-fire and wreathing the sanctuary, thus symbolizes the mystical presence of God among his people and veils the mystery of God from human gaze.

What is true of the mountain of Sinai is true also of the tabernacle. The tabernacle is the local, physical, counterpart of the dwelling of God; every detail of it is in accord with the plan as revealed by God to Moses on the mountain (Exod. 25.9, 40; 26.30; cf. Heb. 8.5; so for the Jerusalem temple, 1 Chron. 28.19). It is doubtless for this reason that the detail of the tabernacle and its furnishings is given exhaustively in Exod. 25.1–31.17 (if, on occasion, confusingly: e.g., in 27.9-18 to have the curtains round the court hung on sixty poles one must assume they are hung as on yard-arms) and that the execution of the tabernacle in accordance with this specification is minutely and with apparently redundant repetition recorded in Exodus 35–40. As the mountain is the place where the LORD descended in his theophanic cloud, so in the cloud his glory fills the tabernacle (40.34ff.).

But characteristic features of the Israelite concept of the sanctuary prevail. Alongside the tabernacle the tent of meeting (Exod. 33.7-11) somewhat confusingly remains: revelation in communicable terms continues alongside the ineffability of the mysterious glory of God in the tabernacle. The sanctuary is no localized temple but a movable shrine which dictates the movements of the people. While much of the detail of the structure and furnishings of the tabernacle (and especially of its model the Jerusalem temple, e.g. the tripartite strucutre of holy of holies, holy place, court corresponding to the 'three decker' universe) probably reflects cosmic symbolism, the presentation, beginning with the ark for the stones of the 'testimony' (25.10ff.) and ending with the stipulations for the observance of the sabbath (31.12-17), emphasizes distinctively Israelite beliefs.

Further Reading

A. Biran, ed., *Temples and High Places in Biblical Times* (Proceedings
of the Colloquium in Honor of the Centennial of Hebrew
Union College, Jerusalem, 1977), Jerusalem: Hebrew
Union College-Jewish Institute of Religion, 1981.
B. Otzen, 'Heavenly visions in early Judaism: origin and function',
in W.B. Barrick, J.R. Spencer, ed., *In the Shelter of Elyon*
(Ahlström Festschrift), JSOTS 31, 1984, 199ff.

V. Covenant

'Covenant', by which the relationship between God and people is
formally defined in Exod. 19.1–24.11; 34.1-28, provides yet another
example of the process whereby an institution practised widely in the
ancient Near East in both space and time has been secondarily
associated with exodus/Sinai in such a way that exodus/Sinai is
presented as the original and supreme instance, which thereby
provides that institution with its necessary aetiology. Because of the
demands of the Exodus presentation of Israel's history in a linear
narrative, covenant is focused on Sinai as if it were an event which
happened once for all time. It is, on the contrary, the institutional
commonplace in the ancient world whereby parties not related to one
another by the immediate natural family tie of blood bind themselves
to one another by ties of reciprocal obligation. As such, covenant
belongs to the immemorial customs of the world of Israel's origins.
Only secondarily has it been applied in the Old Testament theologically to denote the relationship between God and Israel.

That 'covenant' at its most elemental is primarily an inter-human
contract can be seen from a number of instances of its usage in the
Old Testament itself. Marriage is obviously one of the simplest forms
of covenant between parties not previously linked to each other by
family ties (Mal. 2.14). A solemn agreement between two friends can,
equally, be termed a covenant (1 Sam. 23.15-18). Two passages in
particular, Gen. 31.43-54 and Jer. 34.8-22, provide information about
the rites involved in covenant-making between human parties and
their significance. Both concern parties not linked to each other by
ties of immediate family: Jacob and Laban, though related to each
other as nephew and uncle, belong to separate households (Gen.
28.2); the slaves of the people of Jerusalem (Jer. 34.8ff.) have been
bought by them into their households. In both cases the two parties

have been thrown into a relationship which requires regulation. There is an objective token that an agreement has been made: the pillar/heap of witness in Gen. 31.45ff. presumably implies that the terms of the agreement between Jacob and Laban are oral; in Jeremiah 34 there may have been an objective document containing the terms of the agreement. The terms are agreed between the two contracting parties and commitment to the terms of the agreement is sworn on oath (Gen. 31.53) or solemnly pledged by a rite of self-imprecation (Jer. 34.18f.). The fact that this commitment is sworn or pledged before God makes God witness to the agreement (Jer. 34.15); his surveillance is now the sanction securing adherence to the terms of the agreement, even in secret, when no human witness is present (Gen. 31.49f., 53); he is the agent of the punishment of the partner who is guilty of breach of the stipulation of the covenant (Jer. 34.17). The agreement is capped, at least in Gen. 31.54, by a common meal at the sanctuary. If table fellowship is the supreme expression of the solidarity of the independent household, the communion sacrifice (the *zebaḥ sh^elamim*) at the sanctuary performs that function for the covenant community. In it the offering is divided between three parties, the offerer, the priest and God (e.g. Lev. 7.11ff.). Through participation in the body and blood of the one sacrificial victim (the formulation is that of W. Robertson Smith), God, his mediators and his people are bound together in the new solidarity, the new blood-tie of the one covenantal relationship, which transcends the old one of the mere kin group.

The background of the covenant ceremony in Exodus, especially Exod. 19.3-9; 24.1-11, is thus a practice of immemorial antiquity, to which many of the details conform—situation to be regulated, conditions, promise, stipulation, oath, record, witness, communion sacrifice, new bond in the body and blood of the one sacrificial animal, meal. It is, therefore, not in the least surprising that parallels to the covenant at Sinai have been found in ancient Near Eastern treaties of the second and first millennia BC. G.E. Mendenhall was the first to popularize the view that the LBA Hittite vessal treaties provide close parallels to covenant texts in Exodus and thus support the Mosaic date of the covenant at Sinai. It is now generally acknowledged, however, that because of the wide diffusion of the treaty form, no straightforward conclusion about the date of the covenant material in the Old Testament is possible. As before, one is struck both by the arbitrariness of the argument (vassal treaties are evidenced among the Hittites in the period of Moses; therefore, the covenant at Sinai understood as a vessal treaty can be defended as Mosaic—but in fact vassal treaties from many other epochs are known) and by the fact that it serves to undermine the uniqueness of the institution, the historicity of which it seeks to defend. Without, then, any compulsion to use the parallels as ammunition in the debate about date, one may be grateful for the enhanced appreciation now available of the six-part structure of the typical ancient Near Eastern treaty: introduction of the speaker; historical prologue; stipulations; the document clause; the gods as witnesses; the sanction of curse and blessing. Against this pattern the individuality of specific texts, not least biblical texts, can be the more clearly perceived. It is evident that, for example, the Deuteronomy material adheres much more closely to this pattern than does that of Exodus.

Much more interesting than the question of date, insoluble as it is by this means, is the observation of the adjustments the category 'covenant' had to undergo in the Old Testament when it was transferred from the normal 'horizontal' inter-human contract *before* God as witness to the 'vertical' axis, to a covenant *with* God as partner. Like all analogies, 'covenant' eventually breaks down. Exodus presents a thorough-going attempt to apply the full rigour of the category to the relationship between God and Israel. Israel is repeatedly given the option of undertaking its side of the agreement; repeated assurances are given that they regard themselves as able to keep the agreement (Exod. 19.8; 24.3). But no sooner is the covenant concluded by the people on the plain (Exod. 24.3-8) and by its representatives on the mountain (Exod. 24.1f., 9-11), than, when the covenant-mediator Moses' back is turned (Exod. 24.12–31.18), the people fall away in the worship of the 'golden calf' (Exodus 32). The covenant is, nonetheless, remade by God on the identical terms as before (Exod. 34.1-28) to declare that though all men should be false yet he will remain faithful. The covenant unilaterally abrogated by man is unilaterally reinstituted by God (see further Chapter 4.II.2 (iii)).

Further Reading

G.E. Mendenhall, 'Ancient Oriental Law and Biblical Law', *Biblical Archaeologist* 17, 1954, 26ff.; 'Covenant Forms in Israelite Tradition', *ibid.*, 50ff.

D.J. McCarthy, *Treaty and Covenant*, Analecta Biblica 21A, Rome: Biblical Institute Press, 1978.

E.W. Nicholson, *God and his People: Covenant and Theology in the Old Testament*, Oxford: Clarendon Press, 1986.

VI. Law

Within the framework of the covenantal ceremony in Exod. 19.1-24.11 there is embedded a law-code (Exod. 20.22-23.19), conventionally termed the 'Book of the Covenant' ('B'), on the assumption that it is the document referred to in Exod. 24.7. It will be argued below that it seems relatively clear that this law-code illustrates yet once more the association with Sinai of a long tradition of Israelite and ancient Near Eastern material which has, in its origin and development, nothing whatsoever to do with exodus/Sinai, in order to supply it with normative meaning, ultimate sanction and appropriate aetiology. The question about the processes whereby this material seems to have become associated with Sinai will conveniently provide a link to the next chapter, which will deal with the literary growth of the book of Exodus.

Even when no external texts were available for comparison, the connection of much of this law with the conditions of the Mosaic age seemed open to question. The legislation concerns, indeed presupposes, a settled community living in houses (22.2, 7f. [Heb. 1, 6f.]), frequenting fixed sanctuaries (23.17, 19), possessing cattle as well as sheep (21.28ff.), fields with their crops, vineyards and olive orchards and the necessary installations for pressing the grapes and olives (22.29 [Heb. 28]; 23.10f.). Because there is no reference to a king, a favourite date ascribed to B has been the 12th-11th centuries BC between the settlement and the rise of the monarchy.

The response that Moses was by divine inspiration legislating for future conditions was countered not so much by the view that such prospective legislation was necessarily impossible—though it was regarded as unlikely—as by the observation that, even granting the biblical sequence, before the legislation in B could be put into practice it was already modified, ostensibly forty years later on the eve of the settlement, by new legislation in Deuteronomy (e.g. on slavery Exod. 21.2-11, cf. Deut. 15.12-18). In the light of such evidence, it is more likely that law in Israel passed through the same gradual process of development and periodic compilation in response to changing conditions as in other cultures and as in later Judaism itself (cf. the compilation of the Mishnah ca. AD 200 and of the

Talmud ca. AD 500 and the continuing development of the 'law of Moses' to the present day).

Since the rediscovery of ancient Near Eastern law-codes, especially the publication in AD 1902 of the law-code of the Babylonian king Hammurabi (ca. 1700 BC; cf. *ANET* 159ff.; 523ff.), it has become clear that there is a long and widespread legal tradition in the ancient Near East with which the Old Testament material shows distinct affinity. The law of retaliation, 'an eye for an eye and a tooth for a tooth' (Exod. 21.24), so often held up as an example of OT barbarism but in fact a means of restricting revenge and of ensuring that punishment fits the crime (in any case in Rabbinic interpretation the punishment is commutable into monetary compensation), has its parallel in Hammurabi 196: 'If a citizen has destroyed the eye of one of citizen status, they shall destroy his eye'. Such evidence, once more, does not prove the historicity of the Mosaic revelation at Sinai: rather, it shows that that legislation is the gathering up in Israelite terms of a long legal tradition, which is in the Old Testament secondarily focused on Sinai. There, by that theological shorthand, it receives ultimate warrant. Later Jewish tradition, which focuses not only the written law but also the oral law on Sinai, can again be compared (cf. e.g. *Aboth* 1.1ff.).

To place the 'date' of B somewhere between settlement and monarchy is simply to be deceived by a misapprehension of the unilinear biblical narrative, as though, if the material cannot be ascribed to the Mosaic period, it must be assigned to a later. Certainly its compilation may be dated to such a period (and there is the tradition in Josh. 24.25 of promulgation of law by Joshua, as there is by Moses, apart from Sinai, in Exod. 15.25). But the roots of the material are to be traced long before the time of Moses in the ancient Near Eastern society of the third and second millennia BC.

The secondariness of the association of the law-code B with Sinai can, in fact, be relatively clearly established. Within B there is a remarkable variety in the formulation of different blocks of material, and these blocks of material have evidently been brought together by redactional activity with a particular purpose in mind. There are four main types of formulation in B:

(1) The 'when. . ., if. . ., then. . .' type, e.g. 21.18f. This is a discursive variety of law which begins with a general situation ('When men quarrel. . .'), introduces particular circumstances ('if the man rises again. . .') and concludes with the appropriate legal sentence ('then. . . he. . . shall be clear. . .'). The whole is expressed

in the third person ('men. . . the man. . . he') and thus adheres to the standard form of legal formulation in the ancient Near East (cf. *ANET* loc. cit.). As belonging to this type there may be identified 21.1-11 (the second person formulation, 'you', in vv.1f. is wholly exceptional in the context and has come in by attraction from the preceding material in 20.26) and 21.18-22.17[Heb.16]. The technical term for this type of legislation is given in the heading of 21.1: *mishpaṭ*, 'ordinance'. This is the variety of law identified by Albrecht Alt as 'casuistic [i.e. case] law'.

(2) The 'whoever' type, e.g. 21.15. This is terse in formulation. It begins with a participle (in the example 'whoever strikes. . . ' [Heb. *makkeh*]) and is expressed in the third person. 21.12-17 and 22.18-20 [Heb. 17-19] belong to this type (21.13f. seems to be a secondary qualification separating manslaughter from murder; the second person 'you' in 22.18 [17] is again a secondary contamination from the surrounding context; cf. 22.21[20]). It may be surmised that the technical term for this type of legislation (assuming it had one) is *ḥoq*, 'statute', inasmuch as 'statute' is frequently paired with the above class, 'ordinance', in the Old Testament (e.g. Exod. 15.25b; Josh. 24.25). 'Statute and ordinance' are tantamount to the Hebrew for 'law-code'.

(3) The 'you (masculine plural) shall not. . . ' type, e.g. 20.23, i.e. a prohibition addressed to the second person plural. A possible technical term for this type would be *mitswah*, 'commandment'.

(4) The 'you (masculine singular) shall not. . . ' type e.g. 20.24, i.e. a prohibition addressed to the second person singular. This is the same form as the Decalogue, or 'ten words' (e.g. Exod. 34.1; Deut. 4.13), hence the technical term for this variety might be *dabar*, 'word'.

Types (3) and (4) are intermingled with one another and stand as blocks at the beginning and end of B. They thus provide B with its outer framework (20.23-26; 22.21[Heb.20]-23.19). Alt combined types (2)-(4) under the term 'apodeictic [i.e. unconditional] law', but it is probable that they should be distinguished from one another in some such way as will be attempted below.

The interrelationship of these blocks of material can be presented diagrammatically as follows:

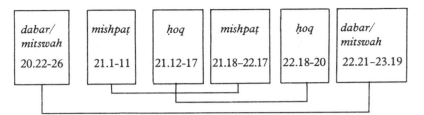

| dabar/ mitswah | mishpaṭ | ḥoq | mishpaṭ | ḥoq | dabar/ mitswah |
| 20.22-26 | 21.1-11 | 21.12-17 | 21.18–22.17 | 22.18-20 | 22.21–23.19 |

What accounts for the arresting fact that the *ḥoq umishpaṭ* ('statute and ordinance') material, formulated objectively in the third person, is held within a framework of *dabar/mitswah* ('word/commandment'), couched as direct second person address? The suggestion may be offered that by the imposition of this framework an original law-code, *ḥoq umishpaṭ*, is being secondarily subordinated to the form of a covenant-code, *dabar/mitswah*, and thereby incorporated within 'covenant at Sinai'.

The *mishpaṭim*, 'ordinances' (21.1-11, 18–22.17[16]), are wholly at home in the age-long legal practice of the ancient Near East. '*Mishpaṭ*' means both 'custom' and 'precedent' as well as the judgement based thereon. The *mishpaṭim* thus cover a wide range of civil and criminal cases (slavery, personal injuries, goring oxen, theft, damage to crops, deposits, loans, seduction, etc.), on which there is established practice. It is striking that in this range of inter-human, mundane, communal issues there is a prevailingly secular tone: there is not a single reference to God as the source of revelation. Neither is it surprising that such issues are not unique to Israel and that the legislation on them has parallels in other ancient Near Eastern law. Jurisdiction in these cases is vested with the 'elders in the gate', i.e. the council of the heads of household within the community alluded to in Exod. 21.22 and more fully described in Deut. 16.18-20; 17.2-7. There is thus an affinity between *mishpaṭ* and wisdom, both in its internationalism and in its chief exponents, the wise men/elders. It is only when the requisite two or three witnesses are lacking that the case must be referred to the sanctuary for decision by the drawing of the sacred lots or affirmation by oath before God (Exod. 22.7-13 [Heb. 6-12]). There is here no primary connection with covenant, let alone Sinai.

The *ḥuqqim*, 'statutes' (21.12-17; 22.18-20[Heb.17-19]) concern actions which threaten the established order of society—the sanctity of the life and freedom of the individual and duty to parents and to God. Infringements of these are absolutely prohibited and necessarily incur the death penalty. Jurisdiction in these matters again belongs to the 'elders in the gate', as the parallel legislation in Deuteronomy on the case of the unruly son makes clear (Deut. 21.18-21; cf. Exod. 21.15, 17). These seven *ḥuqqim* have their counterparts in anathemas pronounced in the curse liturgy in Deut. 27.15-26 but it is clear that that passage is concerned with the prevention of such practices even 'in secret', i.e., when there are no witnesses to bring a case to court. Again there is no necessary link with covenant.

The outer framework elements of *dabar* and *mitswah* (Exod. 20.22-26; 22.21[Heb.20]-23.19), however, introduce a completely new factor: they are expressed not in the objective third person formulation of the law-code but as direct address by God to Israel, both individually and corporately. They are thus cast in the form of the code of the covenant between God and Israel. Naturally, therefore, the stipulations refer to matters directly concerning the divine-human relationship. The opening part of the framework (20.22-26) states the exclusiveness of Israel's relationship to its covenant partner, God, and prescribes the appropriate mode of constructing the altar, the means by which that relationship is expressed and maintained. The materials in the concluding part of the framework (22.21[Heb.20]-23.19) are more miscellaneous in character and are disposed in four sections. Sections one and three (22.21-27[Heb.20-26]; 23.1-9) concern a variety of inter-personal relationships: the care for the weak in society, the stranger, the widow, the orphan, the poor and, even, the domestic animal; the safeguarding of the judicial process—the discharge of *hoq umishpaṭ*— is here taken up into the covenantal obligations. Sections one and three are linked together by the prohibition 'you shall not oppress a stranger', with which section one begins and section three ends (22.21[Heb.20]; 23.9), and by interweaving the humanitarian concern for the domestic animal (23.4f.) with the demand for the upholding of justice. These humanitarian concerns are held within the context of the specific duties of Israel towards God enjoined in sections two and four (22.28-31[Heb. 27-30]; 23.10-19): the prohibition of cursing God; the acknowledgement of God the giver by the offering of Firstlings and Firstfruits; the eating of flesh only if offered according to the approved sacrificial rites; the observance of the sabbatical year, the sabbath and the three annual pilgrimage festivals.

Although all of these are couched in the *dabar/mitswah* form, there are vestiges of the *mishpaṭ* 'when. . ., if. . ., then. . . ' formulation in the regulations for the building of the altar in 20.24f., for lending to the poor in 22.25-27[Heb. 24-26] and for the care of the straying or overburdened beast in 23.4f. These traces may provide valuable evidence for the process here being proposed: material originally a law-code, couched in *ḥoq umishpaṭ* form, is in B being taken up and incorporated secondarily into a covenant-code in the *dabar/mitswah* formulation. If the commonplace institution of covenant itself, within the context of which law is thus placed, is secondarily focused on Sinai as the supreme example from which all other examples derive their significance, then *a fortiori* the focusing of all law on Sinai is still more secondary.

That a process of assimilation of law-code to covenant-code was indeed taking place in the presentation of the Pentateuch is confirmed by a comparison of the Book of the Covenant with the code in Deut. 12.1–26.15. The introduction to the code in Deut. 12.1 is very revealing: there the contents about to follow are termed '*ḥuqqim*' and '*mishpaṭim*' 'statutes' and 'ordinances', though they are almost uniformly cast in the form of second person address, i.e what has begun life as a law-code is now presented as a covenant-code. Thus material which appears in Exodus in the third person *mishpaṭ* formulation of the law-code is reformulated in Deuteronomy in the second person *dabar/mitswah* of the covenant-code (cf. e.g. the legislation on slavery in Exod. 21.2-6 [third person *mishpaṭ* form] and Deut. 15.12-18 [second person *dabar* form]). Exod. 22.21-27[Heb.20-26]; 23.1-9 thus represents an intermediate stage of development in the reformulation of law-code as covenant-code, between the pure *mishpaṭ* form and its full-scale assimilation to the *dabar/mitswah* form in Deut. 12.1–26.15. The basic character of B as a law-code remains essentially unchanged: it has been transformed into a covenant-code by the addition of the outer framework and some small consequential adjustments (especially the second person address which has crept in at 21.1f. and 22.18[Heb.17]). By contrast, Deuteronomy represents a full-scale transformation of law-code to covenant-code, appropriately enough in a book which is widely regarded as the covenant document *par excellence* in the Old Testament.

It would not be surprising if, therefore, the material in Exodus proved itself to be of earlier date than that in Deuteronomy. It is, accordingly, to the question of the comparative date of this material that attention must now be turned. The question of date inevitably involves questions about the origins of the material, the processes of its composition and compilation, the people involved in these processes and the purposes with which they set about their work.

These are the questions which have traditionally in scholarship been gathered together under the heading 'literary criticism'.

Further Reading

The 'classical' study of law in the Old Testament is

> A. Alt, *Essays on Old Testament History and Religion*, Oxford: Blackwell, 1966 (repr. Sheffield: JSOT, 1989), 79ff.

The user should be warned that there are a number of mistakes in this translation of the 1934 German original, e.g. the extent of 'casuistic' law in B should read xxi:2-xxii:16 on p. 88, nn. 15 and 16; in the discussion of the protasis of 'casuistic' law the Hebrew conjunctions *ki* and *'im* have been transposed on p. 89.

> S.M. Paul, *Studies in the Book of the Covenant in the Light of Cuneiform and Biblical Law*, VTS 18, 1970.
>
> H.J. Boecker, *Law and the Administration of Justice in the Old Testament and Ancient East*, London: SPCK, 1980.
>
> D. Patrick, *Old Testament Law*, Atlanta: John Knox, 1985.
>
> R.E. Clements, *Deuteronomy* (Old Testament Guides), Sheffield: JSOT Press, 1989.

3

MATTERS LITERARY:
THE CREATIVE SYNTHESIS

IN THE LIGHT OF the foregoing discussion, it is clear that the book of Exodus represents an extraordinarily rich amalgam of the most diverse materials. It must now be our task to try to trace the literary growth of this collection; our particular concern will be to understand the intentions of those responsible for the various stages of its compilation and redaction. But because Exodus is integrally connected with the other books of the Pentateuch, discussion of its origins and growth cannot be separated from the wider problems of Pentateuchal study.

To open up a way into these questions and the myriad discussions of them, three major contributions to the study of Exodus will first be looked at, those of S.R. Driver, M. Noth and B.S. Childs. Each comes from the hand of a scholar who has written (among his many other works) not only a commentary on Exodus itself but also a work of 'introduction' on the wider issues of Pentateuchal composition and who represents, or has even pioneered, a distinctive approach. Thereafter, two further approaches to the interpretation of Exodus will be looked at: the history of redaction and the literary approach. The chapter will conclude with a study of the Decalogue, as a comprehensive illustration of the issues.

Further Reading

Among the 'myriad discussions' available in English, besides those to be studied more closely below, the following may be noted.

Introductions:

> O. Eissfeldt (1965), R.K. Harrison (1970), G. Fohrer (1970), O. Kaiser (1975), J.A. Soggin (2nd edn, 1980), W.H. Schmidt (1984), R. Rendtorff (1985).

For a review of the issues involved in such works see:

> R.E. Clements, *A Century of Old Testament Study*, 2nd edn, Guildford: Lutterworth, 1983.
> J. Barton, *Reading the Old Testament*, London: Darton, Longman & Todd, 1984;
> J.H. Hayes, C.R. Holladay, *Biblical Exegesis: A Beginner's Handbook*, 2nd edn, London: SCM, 1987.
> R.N. Whybray, *The Making of the Pentateuch: A Methodological Study*, JSOTS 53, 1987.

Commentaries: Further technical commentaries on the Book of Exodus (leaving aside smaller ones of a more confessional, devotional or homiletical nature) include

> J.P. Hyatt (New Century Bible, London: Oliphants, 1971), conceived largely in traditional 'literary critical' terms (cf. Chapter 3.I);
> J.I. Durham (Waco, Texas: Word, 1987), an essay in 'final form' interpretation (cf. Chapter 3.V).

For an evaluation of selected recent commentaries on Exodus, see

> C.S. Rodd, 'Which is the Best Commentary? VIII. Exodus', *ET* 98, 1986/7, 359ff.

The large commentary by W.H. Schmidt (1974ff., of which only the first fascicles have so far appeared) in the full-scale German series, Biblischer Kommentar, must also be mentioned. It is cast in the 'form-critical/history of tradition' mould (cf. Chapter 3.II). Cf. his

> *Exodus, Sinai und Mose*, Erträge der Forschung 191, Darmstadt: Wissenschaftliche Buchgesellschaft, 1983.

I. S.R. Driver and 'literary criticism'

Driver's *Introduction to the Literature of the Old Testament* (Edinburgh: T. & T. Clark) was first published in 1891 and passed through nine editions. It became the standard work in English on the subject for two or three generations and helped to secure the ascendancy of a view of the composition of Scripture which had been developing, particularly on the Continent, since the end of the 18th century and even earlier. His commentary on Exodus appeared in the Cambridge Bible for Schools and Colleges (Cambridge University Press) in 1911.

1. *The literary criticism of the Hexateuch*

Because the view of the whole affects the understanding of the part, it is necessary to begin by outlining Driver's general argument in support of the conclusion that it was perhaps not until the 4th century BC that the Hexateuch (he includes Joshua along with the Pentateuch) after a long literary history finally reached its completion and cannot, therefore, have been written in its final form by Moses.

The book of Deuteronomy (on which Driver as joint editor wrote the first International Critical Commentary in 1895) provides the clearest evidence of this, e.g.:

(i) Deut. 34.5f. records the death of Moses;

(ii) Deut. 1.1; 2.12; 3.8 imply that the settlement in Canaan has already taken place—but Moses, according to Deuteronomy 34, died before the settlement;

(iii) the unprecedented measures of Josiah's reformation in 621 BC (especially the centralization of the cult and the mode of celebration of the Passover, 2 Kgs 22f.) match Deut. 12; 16.1-8;

(iv) by contrast, the plurality of altars in the pre-monarchic and early monarchic period, at which Israel's accredited religious leaders functioned uncondemned, shows that the legislation in Deut. 12.1ff. on the one legitimate altar was not yet in existence;

(v) the legislation in Deut. 17.14-20 on the post-Mosaic innovation of the monarchy reflects the account of the reign of Solomon in 1 Kgs 10.28f.; 11.1ff.;

(vi) other laws in Deuteronomy (tabulated in *LOT*, 9th edn, 73ff.), e.g. on slaves and levites, stand midway between the Book of the Covenant in Exod. 20.22ff. and legislation in Leviticus and Numbers.

On the basis of these and many other observations, Driver espoused the 'New Documentary Hypothesis', which had been finally put forward in magisterial synthesis by J. Wellhausen in the 1870s. According to this, the Hexateuch comprises four main literary documents: J (which uses the Divine name 'Jahweh', comes from Judah and is dated in the 9th century), E (which uses the Divine name 'Elohim', comes from Ephraim and is dated somewhat later), D (i.e. Deuteronomy, dated 7th century) and P (the priestly document, dated 6th-5th centuries). These documents were progressively integrated by three redactors, R[JE], R[D] and R[P], in the early 7th, later 7th and 5th/4th centuries respectively. In anticipation of the discussion in Chapter 3.IV, it may be noted that these four 'sources' are not identified with equal certainty: D and P are clear in language, content and date, but J and E are less so.

2. *The literary criticism of the Book of Exodus*

Driver's account of the literary growth of Exodus itself is, accordingly, in terms of the Documentary Hypothesis. But it must be noted that equal weight is by no means given to each document, nor is there equal certainty about their delimitation. In effect there are essentially two: P, the more certain, and JE in combination. Only a few verses, especially in the Decalogue, are recognized as belonging to R^D (though, as noted below, Driver does regard R^{JE} as akin to Deuteronomy).

Driver's identification of P, the framework for his discussion, may be reproduced: 1.1-5, 7, 13-14, 23-26b; 6.2-7.13, 19-20a, 21b-22; 8.5-7, 15b-19; 9.8-12; 11.9-10; 12.1-10, 28, 37a, 40-51; 13.1f., 20; 14.1-4, 8-9, 15-18, 21a, 21c-23, 26-27a, 28, 29; (15.19;) 16.1-3, 6-24, 31-36; 17.1a; 19.1-2a; 24.15-18a; 25.1-31.18a; 34.29-35; 35-40. I shall register substantial agreement with this delimitation of P in Chapter 3.IV.

Virtually the remainder of the material is apportioned by Driver between J and E. But he has to concede that reliable criteria are not always available for making the discrimination between these two sources. His analysis of e.g. 19.3-24.18 and 31.18-34.28, key passages which will occupy our attention in Chapter 3.IV and VI, is acknowledged by him to be provisional: the Decalogue (20.1-17) and the Book of Covenant (20.22-23.33), though derived from pre-existing written sources, are ascribed to E. 34.18-26, because it is parallel to 23.15, 12, 16-19, is attributed to J. 34.1-4, 10-28 must, then, in Driver's view, be regarded as J's original account of the *establishment* of the covenant at Sinai, which once followed 19.20-25; 24.1-2, 9-10, but which has now been displaced to Chapter 34 by the insertion in its place of the parallel material from E in 20.22-23.33; 24.3-8. In its new position it is used by the compiler to describe the *renewal* of the covenant: the terms of this 'renewed' covenant in 34.11-26 are described as 'ten words' (34.28); 'hence', Driver cautiously notes, 'it has been supposed that these verses, though now expanded by the compiler, consisted originally of ten commands forming a "ritual decalogue" (as opposed to the "moral Decalogue" of ch. 20)' (LOT, 9th edn, 39).

Driver regards J and E as 'akin to the writings of the great prophets'. The work of the redactor is estimated positively: 'R^{JE}

approximates in both style and character to Deuteronomy' (*Exodus* xi). There is a convergence here towards the position which will be argued for in Chapter 3.IV, below.

3. 'Tradition'—an unanswered question

Though Driver does not claim to write as a historian, he does wish to defend the historicity of at least the outline of the events portrayed in the narrative. The link which he proposes between the events themselves and the relatively late literary sources JE and P is tradition: 'The date at which an event, or institution, is first mentioned in writing, must not. . . be confused with that at which it occurred, or originated: in the early stages of a nation's history the memory of the past is preserved habitually by oral tradition; and the Jews, long after they were possessed of a literature, were still apt to depend much upon tradition' (*LOT*, 9th edn, 125).

But Driver has left us little indication about how these traditions might have been preserved. One is left with guesses and intuitions as to what the basis and historical content of these traditions might have been. Of Exodus 15, for example, he writes, 'The hyperboles in v.$^{5b.8.10b}$ are too great for an eye-witness, even though a poet, if the crossing took place. . . not in deep water, but in some shallow spot where the wind drove the water aside' (*ibid.* 30). His rationalism cannot be held at bay: progressive tracing of the tradition of the crossing of the Red Sea back through the literary sources leads to progressive naturalistic explanation. 'In. . . E the wonders are greater than in J. . .; . . . in P they are still greater than in E' (*Exodus* liii). But what is gained by reconstructing a less miraculous narrative that is still five hundred years or so after the event? It is precisely in connection with the attempt to trace the history and transmission of traditions from their very origins through to their literary dress that attention now turns to Martin Noth.

Further Reading

R.E. Friedman, *Who Wrote the Bible?*, London: Cape, 1988,

despite its title, is concerned throughout to answer the question, 'Who wrote the Pentateuch?', using literary criticism.

II. **Martin Noth and 'the history of tradition'**

According to the New Documentary Hypothesis, the sources of the Pentateuch, J, E, D and P, reached their definitive literary formulation only in the first millennium BC. But the publication in modern times of thousands of texts from the ancient Near East (e.g. a version of the Babylonian Flood in 1872, the lawcode of Hammurabi in 1902), including some from the second, and even the third, millennium BC, encouraged comparisons with Pentateuchal materials and a reappraisal of the possible antiquity of the traditions lying behind them. It was now becoming clear that these Pentateuchal sources might contain much older written and oral traditions. The technique evolved for tracing these older stages of tradition back from their present literary formulation to their presumed original context in the life of the ancient Near East is broadly termed 'form criticism'. It was pioneered by Hermann Gunkel in the early decades of the 20th century particularly in connection with Genesis and Psalms, for both of which comparative Babylonian material had become available.

'Form criticism' seeks to analyze the literary documents of the Bible into their constituent elements, the individual traditions, and to classify them according to type ('category', *Gattung* or *genre*). The social context (*Sitz im Leben*) of such genres can often be determined, and thus the appreciation of their function within their original social context enhanced (e.g. the Psalm is typically at home in the liturgy of the cult as an expression of national or individual joy or grief; certain types of law are in the hands of the 'elders in the gate'). Form criticism is thus a means of gathering together both biblical and extra-biblical materials of related type for appropriate comparison or contrast. The inner structure of each passage may by this means be the better appreciated, its conventionality or individuality perceived (cf. the discussion on covenant and treaty in Chapter 2.V). It may be possible to propose a 'typology' for a particular genre, i.e. the stages in its historical evolution (*Formgeschichte*, 'the history of the form'), and to locate the individual example in question within that typology (e.g. does a particular Psalm still reflect a specific liturgical occasion or has it developed in form beyond the specifically cultic to become a more universally accessible expression of faith or piety?; is 'covenant' in the Old Testament rightly understood as 'treaty'?). It may thus be possible to trace how and by whom a particular example of a speech form has been transmitted from its original context in the life of the ancient Near East to its present literary formulation in the Old Testament (*Überlieferungsgeschichte*, 'the history of transmission').

The programme of form criticism may be summed up in Gunkel's dictum of 1906: 'Hebrew literary history is... the history of the literary types practised in Israel'. That is, the history of Israel's literature (say, the Pentateuch) must be written not merely by analyzing it into its constituent source documents (in this case, J, E, D and P) and arranging them in historical sequence, as in 'literary criticism'; a more complete account of the literary history of the material will be attained by analyzing these sources themselves still further into their elements and tracing these elements back to their original ancient Near Eastern contexts.

Martin Noth was a major exponent of the form-critical method, especially its history of transmission aspect. A wide-ranging discussion of the issues as they concern the Pentateuch is to be found in his book *A History of Pentateuchal Traditions* (Englewood Cliffs: Prentice-Hall, 1972; original German, 1948). His commentary on Exodus (he also wrote on Leviticus and Numbers) appeared in 1962 (London: SCM; original German, 1959). Noth was also the first editor of the massive Biblischer Kommentar—of which Schmidt's commentary, noted above, is a part—which began to appear in 1955 and is scheduled for completion by the year 2000. The BK may be said to be the carrying through of Gunkel's 1906 programme: to provide a form-critical definition of every pericope of the Old Testament and to trace the history of transmission of the materials therein back to their original *Sitz im Leben*. The aim is to discern the contribution of each pericope of the OT to the overall kerygma of the Bible by means of a thorough account of its origin and development. In this way, precision for the use of the term 'tradition' and as complete an appreciation as possible of the materials transmitted thereby are sought.

Noth, then, defines his task as 'to ascertain the *basic themes* from which the totality of the transmitted Pentateuch developed, to investigate how they were replenished with individual materials, to pursue their connections with each other and to assess their significance' (*HPT*, 3). Access to these materials perforce begins with analysis of the extant literary text of the Old Testament. Noth shows himself in this to be a faithful disciple of the Wellhausenian tradition: P, which is generally easily recognizable, is the basis of the Pentateuchal presentation and has been 'enriched' by JE, just as J, the basis of JE, has been enriched by E. He acknowledges that some passages defy literary critical analysis and cites specifically Exodus 19, 24 and 33 (cf. S.R. Driver). He does allow for a greater presence of D-type material. Since this question will be of some importance in Chapter 3.IV below, Noth's identification of D-style materials in Exodus may be noted: 12.24-27a; 13.1-16; 15.25b, 26; 16.4b*b*, 28; 17.4-7; 19.3b-9a(b); 32.7-14; 33*. 34.1a, 4 are 'secondary'.

But, following a suggestion of O. Procksch, Noth pushes back the development of tradition a stage earlier by postulating that J and E shared a basic text, 'G' (from *gemeinsame Grundlage*, 'shared basis'). He does not decide whether G was written or oral: 'traditio-historically this is not of great consequence'.

In Noth's view, the content of the Pentateuch may be analyzed into five original 'themes': patriarchs, exodus, wilderness, Sinai and settlement. Of these, exodus must be given priority: the 'hymnic' participial phrase 'who brought [you] out [from the land of Egypt]' (Exod. 20.2) is the 'kernel of the whole subsequent Pentateuchal tradition'. The exodus is traced to the 'bedrock' of a historical event, the destruction of the Egyptians in the Sea (Exod. 15.21b). While not all Israel can have been involved in the exodus ('Israel' as an entity only came into being in Canaan), this tradition is so widely attested that many clan elements, later to become part of Israel, must have participated in it. The tradition, or 'saga', first 'emerged, developed and was transmitted' orally by narrators in the pre-state period 'within the anonymous totality of the tribes' when they gathered together on seasonal cultic occasions. On these occasions the hymnic affirmation was recited in the liturgy of the central sanctuary of the tribal league, whose focus was the ark. Thus both the *Sitz im Leben* and the history of transmission of the material have been defined.

In thus stressing the *cultic* context for the development of the basic Pentateuchal themes, Noth was clearly influenced by the form-critical work of Gerhard von Rad. According to von Rad, J, the writer of the earliest Pentateuchal document, based his work on an ancient Israelite confession of faith, 'the short historical credo' still to be found in Deut. 26.5-10, which had its origin in the liturgy of the festival of Weeks at the sanctuary at Gilgal. At that feast, the exodus from Egypt and the conquest of the land were celebrated. A significant point noted by von Rad is that in this confession of faith no mention is made of Sinai. Accordingly he concluded, following an observation already made by Wellhausen, that Sinai constituted a separate tradition (Exod. 19.1–Num. 10.10), preserved in the liturgy of a covenant festival celebrated at the festival of Tabernacles at

Shechem. J used the 'credo' as the framework for his document; he was responsible for the *Einbau* ('inserting') of Sinai into his account of the exodus and conquest, as he was for the *Vorbau* ('prefacing') of the creation narrative of Gen. 2.4ff., and the *Ausbau* ('elaborating') of the patriarchal narrative in Genesis 12ff.

But Noth greatly widened and deepened the discussion. While he preserved the essential institutional dimension of the celebration of Israel's agricultural feasts at the sanctuaries, 'historicized' in terms of the exodus, he rightly criticized von Rad for linking the development of the material on exodus and entry into the land (for Noth they are, in any case, separate 'themes') so narrowly with the offering of first-fruits at just one sanctuary, Gilgal: 'throughout the territory in the pre-monarchic period the tribes had constantly to assert their claim to land. . . Thus the confession that Yahweh willed the possession of the land might have belonged in a rather general way to the presentation of first fruits' (*HPT*, 53).

Noth has thus traced the material back through literary analysis to G, and thence to the oral sources of the basic traditions in the *Sitz im Leben* of the festival celebrations at the sanctuaries. He then considers the subsequent development of the themes at the hands of narrators by the addition of materials of the most diverse character, the origin and growth of which he subjects to similar traditio-historical inquiry. Only a few examples from Noth's extended discussion can be given here. The plague narratives preceding the account of the Passover arose from 'the inventiveness of the storyteller. . . the narrator's impulse to multiply and enhance. . . Events specifically characteristic of Egypt are selected out of a rather general knowledge conveyed by caravan traders of the exotic and interesting in Egyptian life' (*ibid.*, 69). The wilderness wandering was elaborated by the clans and tribes of the southern wilderness 'on the basis of their knowledge of the caravan routes. . . and of local traditions clinging to various stations along the way' (*ibid.*, 116). Sinai is one of these southern traditions. The figure of Moses is linked most strongly to the wilderness tradition; the historical nucleus of the Moses material is the grave tradition in Deut. 34.6, in all probability 'the bedrock of a historical reality which is absolutely original' (*ibid.*, 173). In these elaborations, 'what particularly stirred the interest of the Pentateuchal narrators was. . . not so much unique historical events in the course of living on the land, as the abiding everyday conditions of life' (*ibid.*, 191). The basic themes and the individual traditions were then 'bracketed' together by such means as 'secondary' genealogies and itineraries, as well as by all-pervasive figures, pre-eminently Moses. Then, with the advent of written sources, 'the Pentateuchal narrative moved out of the sphere of the cult essential in the formation of the themes and out of the popular sphere essential in narrative elaboration and entered the *theological* sphere of reflection' (*ibid.*, 228). Noth holds that each of the sources, J, E and P, constitutes a literary work of sustained theological discourse, attributable to an 'author'.

Finally, Noth considers the completed Pentateuch: 'Since the completed Pentateuch is what we have to interpret, and all literary criticism and traditio-historical investigation must be regarded only as a measure for the fulfilment of this task, so a history of Pentateuchal traditions is bound to end up again with the Pentateuch as a whole' (*ibid.*, 248). And not only so in its own terms: 'the literary whole has been read as Holy Scripture and has been used in worship. Therefore it is also a task of scholarship to take into its purview this totality' (*ibid.*, 250).

Further Reading

H. Gunkel, 'Fundamental Problems of Hebrew Literary History', in *What Remains of the Old Testament*, London: Allen & Unwin, 1928, 57ff.

G. von Rad, 'The Form-critical Problem of the Hexateuch', in *The Problem of the Hexateuch*, Edinburgh: Oliver & Boyd, 1966, 1ff.

K. Koch, *The Growth of the Biblical Tradition*, London: A. & C. Black, 1969.

III. Brevard S. Childs and 'canonical criticism'

In BK the last section of the commentary on every pericope seeks to draw together the significance of the passage for biblical theology and thus achieve the aim, expressed by Noth but left, it must be said, rather undeveloped by him, of interpreting the OT as part of Holy Scripture, the book of the believing and worshipping community. There can be little doubt that it has been B.S. Childs who has most vigorously pursued this goal. Childs' commentary on Exodus (London: SCM) appeared in 1974. It has itself no introduction, for Childs has very accessibly set out his theory of interpretation with practical examples in an earlier study, *Biblical Theology in Crisis*

(Philadelphia: Westminster, 1970). (The title refers to the perceived collapse during the 1960s of the 'Biblical Theology Movement', which emphasized to the point of exclusiveness the notion that God reveals himself through his mighty acts in history—preeminently, it is apposite to note in this context, the exodus.) The aims enunciated by Childs in *Crisis* have been exhaustively pursued not only in his commentary but in a further series of volumes including *Introduction to the Old Testament as Scripture* (London: SCM, 1979).

In *Crisis*, Childs makes it clear that he writes fundamentally as a Christian minister, who is concerned to give an account of the *Old Testament* as it actually functions in the church as Scripture, and to further that function. Childs rejects as inadequate the prevailing practice of 'historico-critical' exegesis—the tracing of the origin and growth of an OT text within the life of ancient Israel and against its ancient Near Eastern background (cf. Chapter 3.II). Interesting and illuminating though that often is, the *Old* Testament can be adequately interpreted only along with the New Testament within the context of the canon of the whole Christian Bible, i.e. within a Christian *biblical* theology. He is scathing of modern commentators, e.g. on Psalms, who 'avoid scrupulously any reference to the New Testament while providing every conceivable Babylonian parallel' (*Crisis*, 144).

His argument may be indicated by the following loose catena of quotations. 'The Scriptures continue to point to a living God who spoke through his servants in the past, but who continues to confront the church and the world with his divine will. The Scriptures remain the vehicle through which he communicates afresh to his people by the activity of his Spirit' (*ibid.*, 131). The exegete is, therefore, no mere antiquarian: 'To do Biblical Theology within the context of the canon involves the acknowledgement of the *normative* quality of the Biblical tradition' (*ibid.*, 100). The exegete's task is only accomplished when the individual passage is seen in its theological interrelationship with the whole, i.e. in its 'canonical intentionality' (*Introduction*, 79). The Testaments mutually interpret one another: the NT 'guards the Old Testament from distortion. . . God. . . is not the God of Israel alone, but of all nations. The physical blessings of this world—life, land, the people—are an inheritance that points to the ultimate reward which is God himself' (*Crisis*, 218f.). The 'reverse move. . . has no historical rationale, but rests on the confession of a theological context' (*ibid.*, 109). It is this wider goal which opens the door to the recovery of the rich tradition of interpretation from 'pre-critical' times, especially the Fathers, the Rabbis and the Reformers.

Having stated these principles, Childs goes on to illustrate their application in the commentary (one of the examples in *Crisis* is reproduced directly from *Exodus*, then in process of preparation). The standard critical sections on textual, literary, form-critical and traditio-historical questions are executed with the utmost thoroughness and not a little innovation. But Childs regards his sections on the wider OT and NT contexts, within which the passage now stands by virtue of the canon, and on contemporary theological reflection as the most significant for his overall aim.

The commentary provides a veritable feast of material. The major doubt rests on whether it is possible to achieve all this within the covers of one book. One need not doubt that tasks such as Childs envisages must be tackled in the discussion of the theology of the Old Testament and in biblical theology, as well as in systematic, moral and pastoral theology. The believer as believer must do the best possible within the limits of being an individual to work out a coherent personal stance using the resources of the Bible, tradition and experience to do so. But that is surely a co-operative enterprise. The exegete as exegete has a distinctive, if modest, part to play in that much wider inter-specialist task. The possibilities for relating OT to NT alone fan out into an almost limitless range. Childs has laid down two principles for doing this (*Crisis*, 114ff.): (1) following up the explicit citations of the OT in the NT; (2) exploring passages which appear to be cognate in the semantic range of their vocabulary, especially where explicit quotation is lacking. The second of these may lead the interpreter in myriad directions. If that is true of the relation between OT and NT, it is still more so of the relation of biblical theology to general theology. Indeed, one wonders whether Childs' model for the latter is wholly adequate. That the word of God, prevenient in his world, addresses the world and the church only through the canon as '*the*' vehicle of revelation seems inappropriately restrictive. Childs is in danger of substituting a new dominating biblical theology for the one he perceives as outmoded.

In the remaining sections of this chapter we return to the more restricted matters of run-of-the-mill 'introduction', not least to some questions still outstanding from those raised by Noth.

Further Reading

Childs' challenging proposals have been frequently subjected to appraisal, e.g. in *JSOT* 16, 1980 and

> J. Barr, *Holy Scripture: Canon, Authority, Criticism*, Oxford: Clarendon, 1983, 130ff.

For a slightly different approach, emphasizing canon as organic growth and as model, see

> J.A. Sanders, *From Sacred Story to Sacred Text: Canon as Paradigm*, Philadelphia: Fortress, 1987.

IV. Redaction criticism

1. Further considerations concerning the 'form-critical' approach
Childs finds that much critical work is preoccupied with analysis and the recreation of origins rather than with synthesis and the function of the 'final form' as canon of Scripture. Certainly, despite Noth's protestation about doing justice to the material, the great weight of his inquiry lies on the reconstruction of the earlier stages of the traditions.

(i) In Noth's historical reconstructions there is a high degree of the speculative and arbitrary. There is nothing in principle wrong with speculation: where evidence is sparse, it is essential and potentially creative. But to term Exod. 15.21b ('Sing to the LORD, for he has triumphed gloriously;/the horse and his rider he has thrown into the sea') and Deut. 34.6 ([The LORD] buried him [Moses] in the valley in the land of Moab opposite Beth-peor; but no man knows the place of his burial to this day), with their strongly theological character, the 'bedrock' of historical events is, viewed from a coldly historiographical standpoint, a confusion of categories.

(ii) Equally, Noth's (and von Rad's) account of the literary growth of the Pentateuch, impressive in its sustained argumentation though it is, remains speculative. He is obliged to concede, e.g., 'we must deduce it [the growth of the exodus 'theme'] happened this way even without being able to give evidence in detail' (*HPT*, 51). There is, in any case, room for doubt about the status of the 'themes' in general. The wilderness traditions hardly stem from a basic 'theme' and Noth admits that it has no cultic rootage. It is more likely to be a conglomeration of elements of local knowledge about pilgrimage and caravan routes and desert conditions, combined at the literary level with ideological purpose. One may also question the originality of the theme 'promise to the patriarchs': it could be as well a reading back as a basic building-block. The so-called 'themes' may not be the original traditions which have grown by accretion and aggregation into 'G', but literary constructions formulated late in the history of the material to give narrative coherence to the normative theological account of Israel's origins.

(iii) Noth's contention for the existence of a pre-monarchical 'all Israel' central sanctuary, as the focal point for the gathering of traditions and their normative spread throughout the tribes has also been heavily criticized: such unity may only have arisen with the Davidic monarchy, if then—or, indeed, if ever. The influences and institutions supplying cohesion to the traditions are likely to have been more diffuse: there was a shared history (freedom from Egyptian overlordship, a brief period of autonomy, followed by Mesopotamian domination), a shared social background (the common and diverging interests of shepherd, peasant and urban dweller within an accepted legal and social framework) and a shared set of religious observances (sacrifice, festivals at local sanctuaries), which provided the necessary presuppositions for the construction of the national epic of origins in Exodus. But normative Yahwism, with its definitive interpretation of life during this history under these social conditions and expressed through these institutions, could hardly have prevailed without a hard-fought battle and creative work by dedicated theologians. And indeed it may only ever have prevailed among minority groups: how typical of the people as a whole were the gatherers of traditions during the Babylonian exile, with their interpretation of the past as a tale of the continuous breach of covenant by the community?

(iv) Perhaps there is an analogy between Exodus as a source for the reconstruction of the undoubted history of Israel's forebears in the transition between LBA and IA (see Chapter 1.VI) and Exodus as a source for the reconstruction of the literary history through which the traditions of Israel in their transmission have undoubtedly passed. The Israelites were in some sense 'slaves in Egypt'; but the resources for reconstructing that experience in historiographical detail are not available in Exodus. Similarly, multitudinous traditions were transmitted through multiple channels, no doubt formulated in conventional forms congenial to eventual integration. But one could as well hope to analyze one stream issuing from a vast reservoir into the constituent elements of the waters that have fed that reservoir as to retrace back to their sources the history of the individual elements that went to make up the narrative as it now stands. The task is the more impossible since the narrative represents a highly eclectic selection and combination of masses of commonplace information and institutional data. As Childs has stated, the motivation of the biblical sources is quite other than to given evidence for the reconstruction of the historical processes of their origin and development. The processes undoubtedly took place—and one is entitled to speculate about them to one's heart's content—but the evidence for them is no longer in any way complete, or even largely available, in this collection. This may seem a negative conclusion, but, I believe, as I shall argue below in Chapter 3.IV.2-3, there remains much that the critic can, with great certainty and usefulness, describe.

2. *The history of the redaction of the Book of Exodus*
In the following sections an account of the history of the redaction of Exodus will be given which is more modest in its specific aim than either literary or form criticism, but more ambitious than canonical criticism.

Without denying the possibility of highly complex origins for the material such as literary and form criticism have suggested—indeed, while acknowledging the unfathomability of these origins—redaction criticism concentrates on the later levels of the text where editorial activity and intention can be more certainly discerned. The proposal will be made that it can be established with relative certainty that there are *two main redactions to be found in the Book of Exodus*. The later and final of these is essentially constituted by the material traditionally labelled 'P' by the literary critics, but understood not merely as a *source* so much as an *edition*, which has also provided its own input of material. The non-P material (cf. Driver's JE, R^{JE}, R^{D}) is also to be understood not simply as a source or series of sources but as an earlier edition with its own input of material. It will be argued that this earlier version is best affiliated to the movement which produced both Deuteronomy (the traditional 'D') and the material edited under the inspiration of that movement, conventionally called 'Deuteronomistic' ('Dtr'; cf. especially the 'Deuteronomistic History' [DtrH], which comprises Joshua–2 Kings in the Old Testament). These two editions of Exodus will be referred to, in chronological order, as the 'D-version' and the 'P-edition'.

Redaction criticism will also want to hold its own against canonical criticism. It is not sufficient to interpret Exodus in its 'canonical intentionality' (to use Childs' phrase), i.e. in the sense which is imparted to it by virtue of the fact that it belongs to Christian Scripture. Nor is it enough to concentrate on the 'final' form of Exodus. If it has indeed passed through two successive 'canonical' editions, the D-version and the P-edition, it can only be given its full value if the theological intention of the editors of *both* editions is fully appreciated.

It is thus an erroneous assumption that 'canonical' form is synonymous with 'final' form. The 'final' form of the Old Testament as it now stands has often involved the incorporation of successive 'canonical' forms, the earlier into the later, without abrogation and sometimes even without, or with little, change. The biblical canon is not the result of a single final decision about the canonicity of its contents late in the biblical period when all the materials lay ready to hand. Rather, as a 'rolling' canon, it grew in a complex manner by which collections of earlier materials provided the authoritative nucleus round which by interaction or innovation later materials developed. Simply by affirming 'canon' one does not obviate critical questions. Full appreciation of the content of Scripture must include appreciation of the intention of the editors who, step by step, promulgated authoritative Scripture, so far as that intention can be ascertained. It is that appreciation which redaction criticism aims to achieve.

3. *The Deuteronomistic redaction of Exodus*
Since the existence of a final edition of Exodus (in my terms, the 'P-edition') is self-evident, and since its editorial intention will be studied in Chapter 4.III, this section will concentrate on the more controversial issue of the identification and delimitation of the penultimate 'canonical' version of Exodus, the 'D-version', before its editorial intention too is studied in Chapter 4.

The case for recognizing a D-version underlying the present 'final form' of the P-edition of Exodus may be built up as follows.

(i) There are striking parallels between Exodus and Deuteronomy which suggest that, protruding through the surface of the 'final form' of Exodus, there are outcrops of underlying D material. This is particularly the case in the account of the revelation to Moses on the mountain in Exod. 24.12–34.35. On the basis of the parallel in Deut. 9.7–10.11 one can make the following observations.

(a) The framework of the Exodus material is closely parallel to D (cf. Exod. 24.12, 18b; 31.18; 32.7, 8a, 9, 10, 15a, 19b, 20; 34.1, 4, 28 with Deut. 9.9, 10, 12-15, 17, 18a, 21a; 10.1a, 2a, 3abb, 4a). The standard literary-critical assumption (cf. e.g. S.R. Driver, *Deuteronomy*, ICC, Edinburgh: T. & T. Clark, 3rd edn, 1902, 112, where these parallels are tabulated) has been that Deuteronomy is here dependent on an earlier JE narrative. But the question of the mutual relationship of these two sets of parallels is, in my view, no different from that, for example, between the Deuteronomistic History and Chronicles: that is, these parallel materials come from the same source.

(b) That this framework narrative in Exodus is in fact provided by D is supported by the number of occasions on which the version in Deut. 9.7ff. can be seen to *supply the original form* for the Exodus material, which has subsequently been modified by the final redactor, P. This seems to be particularly clear in the following instances.

(1) Exod. 31.18. The parallel in Deut. 9.10a suggests that the Exodus passage originally read, 'And the LORD gave Moses [1] the two [2] tables of stone written with the finger of God'. The final editor P has added at [1] 'when he made an end of speaking with him upon Mount Sinai' (D uses 'Horeb', not 'Sinai') and at [2] 'tables of the testimony'.

(2) Exod. 32.15a. The parallel in Deut. 9.15 suggests that at the very least it was 'the two tables of the covenant', not 'the two tables of the testimony' which were in Moses' hands.

(3) Exod. 34.1-4. The parallel in Deut. 10.1-3 suggests that the Exodus passage originally read, 'The LORD said to Moses, "Hew two tables of stone like the first, [and come up to me on the mountain, and make an ark of wood,] and I will write on the tables the words that were on the first tables, which you broke [1] [, and you shall put them in the ark]." So he [made an ark of acacia wood and] hewed two tables of stone like the first, [2] and went up the mountain [3] with the two tables in his hand.' P has suppressed the material in square brackets, the construction of the ark, at this point, since he gives it full coverage elsewhere (Exod. 25.10ff.; 37.1ff.). He has added material which matches his own preoccupations—at [1]: 'Be ready in the morning, and come up in the morning to Mount Sinai, and present yourself there to me on the top of the mountain. No man shall come up with you, and let no man be seen throughout all the mountain; let no flocks or herds feed before the mountain', at [2]: 'and Moses [N.B. that 'Moses' is misplaced here, a fact not apparent from RSV] rose early in the morning', at [3]: 'of Sinai, as the LORD had

commanded him, and took' (the circumstantial clause 'with the two tables...' now modified as a verbal clause 'and took the two tables...').

(4) Exod. 32.20b, the account of P's rites consequent to the destruction of the golden calf, entirely replaces Deut. 9.21b.

(5) Exod. 32.25-29 gives P's entirely different account of and location for the vocation of the Levites from those in Deut. 10.8.

(6) These more certain cases make it likely that Deut. 9.9 supplies the original form of Exod. 24.12, 18b: 'The LORD said to Moses, "Come up to me on the mountain and wait there; and I will give you the tables of stone, [the tables of the covenant which I have made with them]." And Moses [remained] on the mountain forty days and forty nights'. P has turned the emphasis on covenant into one on law, hierarchy and theophany by the modification of Exod. 24.12b and the insertion thereafter of vv. 14-18a. (The figure of Joshua in Exod. 24.13 is Deuteronomistic.)

(ii) By a similar process of argument, Deut. 4.10-15; 5 enables the D-version of the theophany, revelation of law and covenant at Horeb (the name of the mountain is preserved in Exod. 33.1-6) to be recovered in Exod. 19.1-24.11.

According to the D scenario, Moses' task is to muster the people to the foot of the mountain, where the 'Ten Commandments' are spoken directly to them out of the awesome fire and other accompaniments of theophany as the basis of the covenant relationship between God and people. Thereafter, Mose alone draws near to receive 'all the commandment and the statutes and the ordinances' (Deut. 5.31; cf. 4.14, 'statutes and ordinances'), which he then mediates to the people. Such a sequence of actions can be relatively easily (*pace* Driver and Noth!) recovered in Exod. 19.3-9, 16-17, 19; 20.1-23.33; 24.3-8).

This is not to say that all these materials were *composed* by the D-redactor, merely that they were *compiled* by him. As argued above in Chapter 2.VI, the law-code of the Book of Covenant (Exod. 20.22-23.33) has a long history behind it: but it can now be affirmed that it was the D-redactor's contribution to remould it as a covenant-code. The D-redactor has not only recast it in its present form but has provided it with its very name, 'the Book of the Covenant' (Exod. 24.7), and has set it and the theophany within the framework of covenant-making (Exod. 19.3-9; 24.3-8). Many characteristic turns of phrase confirm this framework as D (e.g. Exod. 19.5a, 'Now therefore, if you will obey my voice and keep my covenant'; cf. Deut.

11.13; 15.5; 27.10; for Exod. 19.5b, 'you shall be my own possession among all peoples', cf. Deut. 7.6; 14.2; 26.18). The unique altar rites of covenant-making in Exod. 24.3-8 may have some admixture of P-redaction in them, especially vv. 6 and 8a, which resemble P's consecration rites (cf. Lev. 8).

(iii) That the penultimate redaction of Exodus should be termed 'Dtr' (Deuteronomistic) rather than simply 'D' (Deuteronomic) is indicated in a number of places in the Horeb pericope (as we should now call it in the D-version) (cf. the comment on Exod. 24.13 above).

(a) The promise (and implied threat) at the conclusion of the Book of the Covenant (Exod. 23.20-33), which corresponds to the blessing and curse of the covenant in the full-scale D presentation of covenant in Deuteronomy 27-28, includes that of the presence of the angel to lead the people into the land, if they will be obedient (cf. Exod. 33.1-6). This promise is explicitly taken up in thought and expression in Judg. 2.1-5, which is the epilogue precisely to DtrH's account of Israel's actual experience at the entry into the land.

(b) In the incident of the golden calf, the people acclaim their new idol as 'These are your gods, O Israel, who brought you up out of the land of Egypt!' (Exod. 32.4, 8). The odd plural 'gods', given that there was only one golden calf in the exodus narrative, is a deliberate cross-reference to the DtrH account of the golden calves set up by Jeroboam I at Bethel and Dan (cf. 1 Kgs 12.28, where the acclamation is repeated virtually verbatim). For DtrH 'the sin of Jeroboam son of Nebat which he made Israel to sin' in setting up the schismatic and apostate northern kingdom was a fundamental factor in the ultimate exile of Israel (cf. the veiled reference to the exile in Exod. 32.34). This signal and emblematic apostasy, which by definition negated the entire history of the northern kingdom (cf. 2 Kgs 17.16), is in the golden calf incident in Exodus 32 transposed by the D-redactor to the very origins of the people themselves.

(c) As noted above, D in Deut. 4.10-15; 5 conceives that the covenant was made primarily on the basis of the Decalogue, written by God himself, and refers rather *en passant* to the additional 'statutes and the ordinances'. The Dtr presentation in Exodus, however, gives this latter material full expression by incorporating the Book of the Covenant (Exod. 20.22–23.33). This wider basis is recognized explicitly in Exod. 24.3f. by the reference to 'all the words of the LORD', written by Moses. Similarly, whereas in Deut. 10.1-5, in the remaking of the covenant after the golden calf incident, the

Decalogue again stands in the forefront, in Exodus 34 both Decalogue and Book of Covenant are reaffirmed as the conjoint basis of the renewed covenant: Exod. 34.6-7, 14, 17 is a clear reference to the first 'commandment' of the Decalogue in its D form (Deut. 5.7-10); Exod. 34.18-26 quotes some three-quarters of the end of the Book of the Covenant (Exod. 23.12-19). By the shorthand of a reference to the beginning of the Decalogue and to the end of the Book of the Covenant, the Dtr-redactor in Exodus 34 asserts that all the legal material once given from Exod. 20.1 to Exod. 23.19 as the basis of the original covenant is reconfirmed as the basis of the renewed covenant.

This difference in emphasis between D and the Dtr presentation in Exodus as to the basis of the covenant, whether original or renewed (Decalogue in the forefront in D; Decalogue + Book of the Covenant in the Dtr edition of Exodus), holds the key to the understanding of the much-disputed half-verse Exod. 34.28b; 'And he wrote upon the tables the words of the covenant, the ten commandments'. In its present context, Moses appears to be the subject of the verb 'he wrote'. Since elsewhere it is *God* who writes the Decalogue (Exod. 31.18, cf. Deut. 9.10), it has been argued that either 'the Ten Commandments' is an erroneous gloss here or that the reference is to a quite different set of ten commandments which are to be sought in the previous verses. It is for this reason that a 'Ritual Decalogue' has in classical literary criticism been identified in Exod. 34.17-26, which, because it diverges from the 'E' Decalogue of Exodus 20 (cf. 'Elohim' in Exod. 20.1), must be attributed to 'J' (cf. S.R. Driver in Chapter 3.I.2). This, I submit, is entirely erroneous. As far as content is concerned, there is no decalogue in Exod. 34.17-26, but a citation of the end of the Book of the Covenant. As far as formulation is concerned, once again the Dtr-redactor of Exodus is quoting a source recoverable from Deuteronomy: Exod. 34.1, 4, 28b//Deut. 10.1-4a. The parallel in Deuteronomy makes it quite unambiguous that God himself wrote the Decalogue and that 'God' is the subject of the verb 'wrote' in Exod. 34.28b. The Dtr-redactor of Exodus has, however, incorporated Exod. 34.27 ('Write these words; in accordance with these words I have made a covenant with you and with Israel'), which has no parallel in Deuteronomy, in order to include the Book of the Covenant—the conclusion of which has just been cited—as part of the basis of the renewed covenant. This incorporation referring to words which Moses wrote corresponds directly to the note in Exod. 24.3f. about Moses' writing 'all the words of the LORD', i.e. the Book of the Covenant, as part of the basis of the original covenant. The 'Ritual Decalogue' is thus a chimera that must be laid to rest.

The modesty of the above proposals, despite their apparent complexity, should not go unnoticed: the D-version does *not* represent a 'source' as in classical literary criticism but a more or less visible redaction. As a redaction it no doubt incorporates earlier source materials (legal, historical, folk, institutional and the like); the search for these sources is a legitimate, if highly speculative, enterprize. As a redaction, i.e. a full-scale finished edition, it is not merely combining sources as by a 'scissors-and-paste' method but, receiving and reconceiving the work of its predecessors, it seeks to write fluent sense. This may on occasion require large-scale modification of the source material, while at other times only the slightest touch. It is this fluent sense which justifies the stress on literary interpretations (particularly of the 'final form' of the Old Testament) which have come into such vogue since the 1970s (see Chapter 3.V).

(iv) As for Exodus 1-18, it is once again possible to find in Deuteronomy's distinctive presentation of the topics of the two main sections of these chapters (plagues-Passover-exodus in Exod. 1.1–15.21; the itinerary of Israel through the wilderness to Horeb/Sinai in 15.22–18.27 and its associated chronology) a key which enables an earlier Dtr redactional level to be recovered beneath the final P-edition. It will be convenient (in order to link Exod. 1.1–15.21 to a study of the literary approach in the following section, Chapter 3.V, below) to begin with the latter, briefer, section.

(a) Exod. 15.22–18.27: The route from the Red Sea through the wilderness to Mt Sinai in Exod. 15.22–18.27 (plus the earlier notices in Exod. 12.37; 13.20; 14.2, 9b) corresponds, with some abbreviation, to the itinerary in Num. 33.1-15 (P), which summarizes the data of the final edition of the Pentateuch. Israel moves by stages from Marah to Rephidim. The stages are all marked by the 'murmuring' of the people (Exod. 15.24; 16.2, 7-9, 12; 17.3) and by responses from God in the form of miraculous acts performed by Moses. Chapter 18 then records the appointment of judges.

By contrast, in the historical retrospects in Deut. 1.6ff., Israel moves *straight* from the Red Sea to *Horeb*. It is only *after* Horeb that the choice of judges is made and that the sorry history of rebellion in the wilderness begins.

Exodus

These differences in itinerary between D and P are matched by differences in chronology. According to 19.1 (part of the P itinerary), it has taken Israel at least six weeks from the exodus to reach Sinai. This contrasts with the direct journey of Deut. 1.6ff., which may be confirmed by Exod. 19.4 ('I bore you on eagles' wings and brought you to myself'), already identified as part of the D-version. This raises the question whether the 'three-day journey' to worship the LORD in the wilderness, for which Moses asked the Pharaoh's permission, also belongs to the D-version (Exod. 3.18; 5.3; 8.27[Heb.23]; 15.22).

These observations present a *prima facie* case that the postulated original underlying D-version of Exod. 15.22–18.27 passes from the exodus directly to Horeb, and that its contribution to the history of rebellion in the wilderness is confined to the post-Horeb narrative in Num. 10.11ff. The P-edition, by contrast, has disposed symmetrically around Sinai narratives of 'murmuring in the wilderness' associated with the miracles of the quails (Exod. 16.13; Num. 11.31f.), manna (Exod. 16.15ff.; Num. 11.6ff.), water from the rock (Exod. 17.1ff.; Num. 20.1ff.) etc., partly reusing D-material in the process. Accordingly, while some of the material in Exod. 15.22–18.27 appears to be predominantly P, especially 15.22-25a; 16.1-36, other parts have an admixture of D-material more or less refashioned in this new location by the P-edition (15.25b-26; 17.1-16; 18.13-27). Exod. 18.1-12 may be regarded as an authentic relic of the original D-version which picks up Exodus 2–4 (cf. e.g. 'mountain of God', 18.5, matching 3.12; 19.3ff.) and thus ties the covenant at Horeb in cc. 19ff. with the first part of the book.

(b) Exod. 1.1–15.21: There is a lack in Deuteronomy of the sustained narrative retrospect parallel to material in Exod. 1.1–15.21 (such as is found, we have seen, in Deut. 4.10-15; 5; 9.7–10.11//parts of Exod. 19–24; 31.18–34.28), which would assist in the recovery of the D-version beneath the final P-edtion. But there are other indications.

(1) There are numerous more occasional references in the narrative retrospects of Deuteronomy (and in the wider DtrH, especially Josh. 24) to themes in Exodus which suggest the currency of these themes in D/Dtr circles, e.g. the land flowing with milk and honey sworn to the patriarchs and their descendants (Deut. 1.8, 35; etc.); the descent into Egypt as 70 persons (Deut. 10.22); Egypt as 'house of slaves' (Deut. 6.12); the LORD as the 'God of the fathers' (Deut. 1.21); the LORD hardening the heart of Israel's enemies (Deut.

2.30); the plagues as 'trials, signs, wonders, war, a mighty hand and outstretched arm, terror' (Deut. 7.8, 18f., etc.); the enquiry of the son (Deut. 6.20)/teaching to children (Deut. 4.9, etc.); the pillar of cloud by day and fire by night (Deut. 1.33); the drowning of the horses and chariots of the Egyptians in the Red Sea (Deut. 11.3f.; Josh. 24.6f.).

(2) Especially important is the D material on Passover/Unleavened Bread in Deut. 16.1-8 (and the account of its implementation under Josiah in DtrH in 2 Kgs 22–23) and on Firstlings, which immediately precedes it in Deut. 15.19-23.

(3) It is likely, as argued above, that, by the time of the postulated D-version, the material of B could be presupposed, in particular the final part (Exod. 23.12-19), which is cited in Exod. 34.18-26 as the conclusion of the terms of the remade covenant. This material includes legislation on Unleavened Bread, Passover and Firstlings.

It would seem, then, that a promising place to start in the search for the underlying D-version in Exod. 1.1–15.21 would be the material on Passover, Unleavened Bread and Firstlings in Exodus 12–13. In the light of the revolutionary nature of D's Passover, a rite at the central sanctuary which merges with and dominates Unleavened Bread (cf. Deut. 16.1-8; 2 Kgs 22f.; 2 Chron. 35), the account of the domestic observance in Exod. 12.1-28 is more likely to be P than D. This is supported by a large number of detailed observations: e.g. v. 13 cannot be D; v. 9 may even be anti-D polemic; the referring to Israel as a 'congregation' (vv. 3, 6, 19); the echoes of the language of Leviticus, e.g. in v. 10 (cf. Lev. 22.30) and v. 14 (cf. Lev. 23.41); the use of the spring calendar beginning with a month simply called 'the first' as opposed to 'Abib' (vv. 2, 18). Nonetheless, there are echoes of D material which suggest reuse by P of an underlying D-version, e.g. the eating in haste (v. 11, cf. Deut. 16.3) and, especially, the instruction of the sons (vv. 25-28, cf. Deut. 6.20).

The material of Exod. 12.37-51 has also a distinctly P ring to it: e.g. the itinerary (v. 37) matches that of Numbers 33, which, as has been noted above, contrasts with that implied by Deut. 1.6ff.; the chronology (v. 40) belongs to the final framework of the Pentateuch; the legislation on the Passover (vv. 43-50) again concerns domestic observance, which cannot be D. Nonetheless, again there may be echoes of an earlier D-version in the baking of unleavened cakes in v. 39 and the 'night of watching' in v. 42.

By contrast, Exod. 13.1-16 seems to be characteristically D in, for example, its echoes of the legislation of Deut. 15.19–16.8 and of B

(Exod. 23.12-19//34.18-26); its catalogue of the indigenous population (v. 5, cf. Deut. 7.1); its instruction of the young (vv. 8-10, 14-16).

These observations suggest that the original D account comprised at least Exod. 12.29-36; 13.1-16; from the latter passage the P-redactor may have derived some materials in his refashioning of the account of the Passover as a domestic rite separate from Unleavened Bread.

This D material links closely with the preceding narratives of the plagues. The tenth plague, the slaying of the Egyptian Firstlings both human and animal, links directly to the D association of Firstlings with Passover/Unleavened Bread in Deut. 15.19-16.8. The centralization of the cult in D makes the D legislation on Firstlings as revolutionary as that on Passover: whereas in the Book of the Covenant (Exod. 22.30[Heb.29]) they are offered on the eighth day after birth, presumably at a local sanctuary, in D they have to be saved up for annual offering at the central sanctuary as, in some cases, mature animals (cf. Deut. 15.19). These annual rites are here brought into association with the exodus to give them decisive interpretation; in Exodus these institutions are cast in narrative form for an aetiological purpose ('why do we practise this rite?', Exod. 13.5; cf. 12.25).

But the parallel to the D legislation extends even further: immediately preceding the legislation on Firstlings and Passover in Deut. 15.19-16.8, there is the legislation on the release of Hebrew slaves (Deut. 15.12-18). It is striking that the narrative sequence of Exod. 1.1-15.21 should thus parallel so closely the sequence of the legislation in Deut. 15.12-16.8 on release of Hebrew slaves-Firstlings-Passover. Deut. 15.12-18 (especially, v. 13) contains two key terms which recur in the presentation of the exodus in Exod. 1.1-5.21 as the release of the Hebrew slaves:

—'let go' (*shillaḥ*) is a thematic term in Moses' dealings with the Pharaoh throughout the plague cycle and links back before that to Moses' call narrative (Exod. 3.20; 4.21, 23; 5.1, 2; 6.1, 11; 7.2, 14, 16, 26, 27; 8.4, 16, 17, 24, 25, 28; 9.1, 2, 7, 13, 17, 28, 35; 10.3, 4, 7, 10, 20, 27; 11.1, 10; 12.33; cf. 13.15, 17; 14.5);

—'empty-handed' (*reqam*): the Hebrew slave, having worked for nothing, is to be recompensed on his release. It is in this light that 'the spoiling of the Egyptians' is to be seen (Exod. 3.20-22, where both *shillaḥ* and *reqam* occur; 11.1-3; 12.35f.): Israel is thus recompensed for their labour as slaves.

These observations vastly extend, then, the possible bounds of the

D-version to embrace, as the historical references scattered throughout Deuteronomy already largely imply, much of the material in Exod. 1.1–15.21. They match other inter-linkages: e.g. the recurrent motif 'believing in Moses' (4.1-9, 31; 14.31; 19.9); the motif of the 'first-born' extends back to 4.21-23.

Certain blocks of material in Exodus 1–11 can, by contrast, be identified with a high degree of probability as 'P': e.g. elements of the final chronological and genealogical schemata of the Pentateuch in 1.1-4; 6.14-27. The latter passage, with its interest in the genealogy of Aaron and the priesthood, raises the question of how far the figure of Aaron is integral to the D-version. That Aaron is essential for the Dtr presentation is clear from Exodus 32, cf. Deut. 9.20. But the role he plays in Chapters 1-11 is inconsistent: in 4.16 his task is limited to speaking to Israel, which he does in 4.30, whereas in 7.2 it is to speak to Pharaoh, which never, in fact, happens. One may suspect, then, that 6.28-7.6 is P's doublet of D's 4.13-17. There appear to be other doublets: the sign of Aaron's rod in 7.8-13 parallels Moses' rod in 4.1-5. The revelation of the name 'Yahweh' which precedes both (3.13-19; 6.2-9) is likely to be another such doublet (6.9 contrasts with 4.31). In summary, 1.1-4; 6.2-7.13 may be assigned to P. As before, this attribution may be confirmed by detailed usages, e.g. 'acts of judgement' (*sh^ephaṭim*) 6.6; 7.4; cf. 12.12; Israel referred to as 'hosts' (6.27; 7.4; cf. 12.17, 41, 51). But as before there is reuse of D-material (cf. *shillaḥ* in 6.11; 7.2).

Exodus 1–18, then, gives an excellent example of the complexity of redaction criticism and its difference from old-fashioned literary criticism. The literary critic would wish at this point to be able to include a summary diagram attributing the materials to the 'sources' JE and P. But the above discussion noting the extensive re-use of D-material by P shows that such a diagram is virtually impossible to produce, especially for Chapters 12, 15 (from v. 22) and 16–18. These chapters all contain materials originally present in the D-version of Exodus and Numbers; but they cannot now be simply attributed to D because they have been extensively relocated by P in contexts where they were not present before in that earlier D-version. Yet in their reuse by P they still retain highly recognizable D features, so that to label them simply 'P' would be equally inappropriate to their intrinsic character. There is here both a striking respect for the older version and desire to utilize it and a radical freedom by which these older materials are reformulated to serve new purposes.

By such study the appreciation of the function of the redactor is greatly enhanced. He is no longer to be seen as a mere editor, more or less subserviently bringing pre-existing materials into as harmonious a whole as possible using the P-document as the base and fitting in as much of JE as he can (as—to take a favourite analogy of the old literary critics—Tatian in the second century AD in his Gospel harmony, the *Diatessaron*, used John's Gospel as base into which he fitted the Synoptics). The redactor is, rather, a creative theologian and hermeneut, who seeks through his faithfulness to tradition and his responsiveness to the demands of his people's predicament to set forth a definitive interpretation of their life before God in as accessible terms as possible. It is in the service of this theological creativity and popular access that he employs every appropriate literary art he can muster.

Further Reading

On the continuing controversy about the date of P and about its character, whether it is 'source', 'redaction' or both, see

M. Noth, 'The "Priestly Writing" and the Redaction of the Pentateuch', Appendix to *The Chronicler's History*, JSOTS 50, Sheffield, 1987.

J.G. Vink, *The Date and Origin of the Priestly Code in the Old Testament*, Oudtestamentische Studiën 15, Leiden: Brill, 1969, 1ff.

F.M. Cross, 'The Priestly Work', in *Canaanite Myth and Hebrew Epic*, Cambridge, Mass: Harvard UP, 1973, 293ff.

D.R. Hildebrand, 'A summary of recent findings in support of an early date for the so-called Priestly material of the Pentateuch', *Journal of the Evangelical Theological Society*, 29, 1986, 129ff.

K. Koch, 'P—kein Redaktor!', *VT* 37, 1987, 446ff.

For a highly complex redactio-historical argument for a Dtr edition of the Pentateuch, see

B. Peckham, *The Composition of the Deuteronomistic History*, Harvard Semitic Monographs 35, Atlanta: Scholars Press, 1985.

V. The literary approach

It is perhaps this awareness of the skill and design of the final redactor as literary artist, coupled with a sense—justified or not—of diminishing returns in traditional criticism, that has awakened intense interest in the Bible as literature among interpreters especially since the 1970s.

A number of terms are applied to this literary approach. It is called 'synchronic'; i.e. the text is considered as a whole, as a concerted literary work with its own artistic integrity, composed, as it were, contemporaneously under a unitary creative impulse. 'Synchronic' is opposed to 'diachronic', i.e. the customary critical analysis, such as has been outlined in the earlier sections of this chapter, which seeks to trace the development of the text through time from its origin, through its manifold redactions to its present composite form. Since synchronic study is applied to the text in its completed form, it is also referred to as 'final form' interpretation. This synchronic study is often concerned with the 'text itself', as a literary creation or artefact. It is the 'text itself' which is the focus of interpretation, not the historical background, the author's intention, the objective realities to which it refers, nor the theological affirmations which it makes. The work is the bearer of, indeed *is*, its own meaning and can be appreciated without reference to the purpose or beliefs of the writer, who may become a figure of no more importance for the appreciation of the artefact than is the painter, sculptor or composer for the appreciation of other works of art.

The plague cycle in Exod. 7.14–11.10 provides within limited compass an interesting case-study for these issues (it has, as has been indicated above, interconnections with both preceding and succeeding materials, so that larger complexes up to and including the complete D-version of Exodus not to say the Pentateuch, not to say DtrH, not to say the final editions of all these, may equally legitimately be studied from this point of view).

Here the traditional literary critical attribution of certain of the plagues or of their elaboration to 'P' rather than 'JE' (cf. Chapter 3.I.2, above) can hardly be said much to heighten understanding. It might be possible, e.g., to begin from the problem of the role of Aaron in Exod. 1.1–15.21, which has been noted above. It could be argued that still more of the material on Aaron should be attributed to the P-edition: if the narrative of Aaron's rod and his contest with the magicians of Egypt in 7.8-13 is regarded as P-material, then all references to his rod and to such a contest might then be held to belong to the P-material; thus, the references to Aaron and the Egyptian magicians in 7.19ff.; 8.1ff., 12ff.; 9.8ff., i.e. in plague narratives 1, 2, 3 and 6. The very phenomenon of this distribution may suggest, however, that there is an alternative, literary, explanation: the figure of Aaron and his rod is being deliberately introduced by the writer into the narrative for specific effect. It is this kind of literary question, which ponders the possibility of the deliberate construction of plot over an extended narrative, that has occupied increasing attention among interpreters.

A literary study of the passage taken as a whole discloses in the regular recurrence of narrative elements the artistry with which it has been structured so that its impact is heightened and its content enhanced. Because of the recurring elements of the drama of confrontation—between the Pharaoh and his officials, on the one hand, and God and his spokesmen and agents, on the other— throughout the ten plagues, and of the stereotyped formulae in which it is cast, it is relatively easy to construct a table (tables and diagrams are recurrent features of the method) of the elements present in principle, and of the extent to which they are represented in each scene. A complete scene would include both the commissioning of Moses to unleash a plague, with instruction about the accompanying message of command and threat to be delivered to Pharaoh, and an account of the carrying out of the commission—the unavailing command and threat, the unleashing of the plague, the temporary relenting by Pharaoh followed by the hardening of his heart.

From such tabulation some obvious points on the subtle arrangement of the plot elements, scene by scene, can be made. No scene is in fact recounted in its required fulness: e.g. there is never an account of both the commissioning and the implementation. Usually the commissioning does duty for both, except in plagues 8-10 where, at the climax of the series, the narrative rushes straight into the action. There is plot acceleration in the very short accounts of plagues 3 (gnats, 4vv.), 5 (plague on cattle, 7vv.), 6 (boils, 5vv.) and 9 (darkness, 9vv.), and retardation by the long accounts especially of plagues 2 (frogs, 15vv.), 4 (flies, 13vv.), 7 (hail, 23vv.) and 8 (locusts, 20vv.). The increasingly frantic concessions by the Pharaoh avail nothing against the inexorable hardening of his heart by the LORD. As for Aaron, he is a wholly subordinate figure. He appears as Moses' agent only when the magicians appear as Pharaoh's accomplices. When by plague 3 these have been outplayed by Aaron, both they and he disappear, except for their brief attempted come-back in plague 6, when they are finally outfaced by Moses himself. Yet only in plague 5 is there no mention at all of Aaron, even by implication.

Perhaps one can agree with those who favour a literary approach that in a passage like this on the ten plagues, the cumulative dramatic impact of the narrative 'as it is' renders highly marginal the question whether the material must have belonged as it stands to the D-version, or even earlier versions, or whether it has undergone limited expansion in the P-edition. Nonetheless, it is damaging to assume that because of a method's clear success in one passage, it is to be absolutized as *the* method throughout. The full range of methods must still be tried passage by passage in order to benefit from any illumination which each may bring.

There is no need to polarize methods. For the community of synagogue and church, scripture is used not merely for aesthetic satisfaction, though there is no reason why that should not bulk largely; it is read because it is assumed that it provides access beyond itself to theological truth and to religious experience. Authorial and editorial intention remains one, if not the sole, means by which theological significance is communicated. (Even in the appreciation of art, for example, knowledge of background, genre and artist's view-point may be vital: it is not unimportant for the appreciation of, say, Camille Pissarro's rural scenes to know that he was an Impressionist with left-wing political views.) Nor is there need to regard 'synchronic' and 'diachronic' study as mutually alien. They may function complementarily. The 'diachronic' analytical work outlined in Chapter 3.IV may succeed in establishing that there are at least *two* 'synchronic' levels within Exodus: the D-version and the P-edition, *both* of which are worthy of full appreciation, including aesthetic. Further, diachronic study may serve to confirm the confines of the compositional unit, the artistic integrity of which is under study. Without this confirmation, there can be as much of the speculative and subjective in 'final form' interpretation as in the attempt to reconstruct origins and development; one may be just as oppressed by the arbitrariness with which passages are delimited by this kind of study and by the impressionism of the 'reading' offered by it as by the speculations of old-style literary and form criticism.

Further Reading

Essays on the narratives in Exodus 1-14:

C. Isbell, A.M. Vater and D.M. Gunn in D.J.A. Clines, D.M. Gunn, A.J. Hauser, eds. *Art and Meaning: Rhetoric in Biblical Literature*, JSOTS 19, Sheffield, 1982.

Of more general works one might mention

R. Alter, *The Art of Biblical Narrative*, London: Allen & Unwin, 1981.

T.L. Thompson, *The Origin Tradition of Ancient Israel, I: The Literary Formation of Genesis and Exodus 1-23*, JSOTS 55, Sheffield, 1987.

VI. The Decalogue as illustration of the issues

The Decalogue provides a compendious example of the issues in Pentateuchal criticism and appropriately rounds off this chapter.

1. *Literary criticism*

The existence of two recensions of the Decalogue (Exod. 20.2-17, Deut. 5.6-21), a 'doublet', makes possible that comparison of texts which is a staple element in literary criticism.

Between these two versions there are, in fact, some twenty-five variations. These range from mere alternative forms of writing, with no significance for meaning, to matters of considerable substance. Only the most significant variations can be noted here.

There is a difference between the two versions in the way in which the 'Ten Commandments' as a whole are counted: in Deuteronomy the MT supplies ten paragraph dividers (at the end of vv. 10, 11, 15, 16, 17, 18, 19, 20, 21a, 21b; so in Catholic and Lutheran usage), whereas in Exodus there are only nine (the equivalent of the divider between Deut. 5.21a and 21b is omitted; to recover 10 it is assumed that Deuteronomy's first commandment is divided into two; cf. Protestant usage). (Incidentally, a fundamental point for understanding the Decalogue is provided by the Jewish tradition which counts the so-called 'prologue' (Exod. 20.2) as the first 'commandment'. The objection that the prologue is a statement, not a commandment, makes the point admirably: who said they were 'commandments'?— the Hebrew calls them 'words', i.e. 'organizing principles', of which the fundamental one is God's act of liberating his people.)

Within the individual 'commandments' there are differences of detail (the 'commandments' are referred to below by the Roman numerals I-X, following the Exodus system):

II —Deut. 5.8 means 'an image, i.e. any likeness'; Exod. 20.4 reads 'an image *and* any likeness', in order to provide a referent for 'to *them*' (v. 5a), now that II is separated from I; in Deut. 5.9 'to them' refers to 'other gods' (v. 7).

—Deut. 5.9 means 'upon sons [i.e. those of the second generation], and upon those of the third generation, and upon those of the fourth generation'; Exod. 20.6 means 'upon sons [i.e. descendants], even of the third and fourth generation'.

IV —Deut. 5.12 'keep' stresses obedience to a command; Exod. 20.8 'remember' refers to the liturgical re-presentation of an original event.

—The phrase 'as Yahweh your God commanded you' (Deut. 5.12, 16) is added because Deuteronomy purports to be Moses' farewell address recalling the events at Horeb forty years earlier.

—The motive for the Sabbath command in Deut. 5.14f. is humanitarian and based on the mighty acts of God; that in Exod. 20.11 is based on the creation ordinance of Gen. 2.2-3.

VII–X —Deut. 5 adds 'and' at the beginning of vv. 18, 19, 20 and 21 and at 21b, thus not only making *two* prohibitions out of v. 21 but linking the series from v. 17 into a self-contained group of six.

IX —Deut. 5.20 reads 'witness of vanity', picking up the wording at the end of v. 11 on the misuse of the Divine Name; Exod. 20.16 reads 'lying witness'.

X —Deut. 5.21a transposes 'your neighbour's wife' to the beginning of the list and makes of it an independent prohibition.

—Deut. 5.21b uses a different verb 'to covet', in order to mark the independence of the prohibition by its reckoning.

What is one to make of these divergences? The standard literary critical assumption has been that the variations between the two versions suggest that there has been secondary expansion of a common original, which was probably couched in the terse, uniformly negative, form of the present VI-IX, e.g. J.E. Carpenter, G. Harford-Battersby, *The Hexateuch*, London: Longmans, Green & Co., 1900:

I   Thou shalt have none other gods before me.
II Thou shalt not make unto thee a graven image.
III Thou shalt not take the name of Yahweh in vain.
IV Thou shalt not do any work on the seventh day.
V   Thou shalt not treat thy father and mother with disrespect.

VI	Thou shalt do no murder.
VII	Thou shalt not commit adultery.
VIII	Thou shalt not steal.
IX	Thou shalt not bear false witness against thy neighbour.
X	Thou shalt not covet thy neighbour's house.

A typical view (Carpenter and Harford-Battersby again) would be that, though the Decalogue in Exod. 20.2-17 now appears in the E document (cf. 'Elohim' in Exod. 20.1, 19), it is a secondary adition to it: E already has its own material parallel to I-IV (for I cf. 22.20[Heb.19]; 23.13; for II cf. 20.23; for III cf. 22.28[Heb.27]; for IV cf. 23.12). The Decalogue is thus likely to be later than E (just as it is later than J, which has its own equivalent to II in 34.17). But equally it is earlier than D, which presupposes it in Deut. 5.6ff. Nonetheless, it is a significant concession that even in its Exodus form the Decalogue has undergone D expansions in the prologue (original form, 'I am Yahweh which brought thee out of the land of Egypt'), in II ('a jealous God, visiting the iniquity of the fathers upon the children, upon the third and upon fourth generation of them that hate me and showing mercy unto thousands', cf. 34.7, 14), in IV (Exod. 20.9-10; Exod. 20.11 = R^P), in V and in X. *OH* thus dates the basic form of the Ten Commandments in the seventh century, between JE and D.

This conclusion is thoroughly in line with the view of the history of Israel's religion in the classical literary criticism of the Wellhausenian type: the Decalogue is dependent on the work of the great eighth century prophets, who were the founders of ethico-religious monotheism.

2. *Form criticism*

OH is notably vague in its account of the origins and social setting of the Decalogue. A number of attempts in the second and third quarters of the 20th century to answer such questions more effectively by means of form criticism may be mentioned.

(i) S. Mowinckel, *Le Décalogue*, EHPR 16, Paris, 1927: In the first two chapters of this work, Mowinckel considers the traditional literary critical questions. He concludes that the Decalogue was composed in the latest pre-exilic period between Isaiah and Deuteronomy. It was incorporated into Deuteronomy about 600 BC by a D redactor. It was then introduced about 500-450 BC by R^{JEDP} into the framework of E, which originally passed directly from Exod. 19.19 to 20.18.

Mowinckel's third chapter, where he turns, expressly following Gunkel's method, to inquire into the form, function and *Sitz im Leben* of the Decalogue, marks a definite advance in the consideration of the historical and social questions.

Mowinckel has already argued that from Exod. 34.17-26 and 20.22-23.19 respectively one can identify J and E cultic Decalogues, which go back to a common original. The form of these Decalogues he identifies as the priestly *torah*, the ruling on who may enter to participate in the rites of the Jerusalem Temple (cf. the 'Entrance Liturgies' preserved in Psalms 15 and 24).

The particular occasion on which this type of material functioned as 'entrance liturgy' is the autumn new year (cf. e.g. Lev. 23.23ff.), which, Mowinckel argued, was a festival of covenant renewal. The evidence for this argument comes primarily from Psalms, especially Psalms 99, 81, 95, 50. Such Psalms, though late in their present form, arose as liturgical texts. Psalm 81 appears to be particularly significant: v. 3[Heb. 4] refers to a pilgrimage festival, which, because of the mention of the sounding of the trumpet, must be the autumn festival (cf. Lev. 23.24); v. 6[Heb. 7] celebrates the exodus, v. 7[Heb. 8] the wilderness wandering to Kadesh, v. 8[Heb. 9] the giving of the law, v. 9[Heb. 10] echoes I and II (Exod. 20.3, 5), v. 10[Heb. 11] the prologue (Exod. 20.2), a reflection of ancient Near Eastern royal speech convention, which marks the 'epiphany' or 'parousia' of Yahweh. The priestly *torah* is thus 'brought into relation with the announcement made by a [cultic] prophet of the epiphany of God who comes to renew the covenant'.

The primary form of the present Decalogue, underlying the accretions of the D and P schools, is, according to Mowinckel, due to the circle of Isaiah's disciples (cf. Isa. 8.16). The Decalogue was the 'entrance liturgy' to their circle, made necessary because of their rejection of customary mores, both popular and official.

(ii) A. Alt's form-critical work has already been noted in Chapter 2.VI. He differs from Mowinckel in two important respects: (1) in his view, the Decalogue functioned not as 'Entrance Liturgy' but as the central text proclaimed by the Levites, on the basis of which the covenant was renewed; (2) these texts were proclaimed, not every year, but every seventh year, i.e. the sabbatical year, when the ground was left fallow and debts were cancelled. But this kind of law is not limited to the cult: 'it displays an unrestrained... aggression which seeks to subject every aspect of life... to the unconditional domination of the will of Yahweh; it pursues the Israelite out of the sanctuary. . . into his daily life' (*op. cit.*, 132).

On the question of the date of such apodeictic material as the Decalogue, Alt is of the opinion that it goes back at least in form to the period when Israel's relation with the LORD was first understood in terms of a covenant, i.e. to the desert period. Alt is unimpressed by the traditional literary critical argument that the Decalogue is dependent upon the work of the 8th century prophets. Nonetheless, he acknowledges that the present formulation of the Decalogue is likely to be much later: cf. its prosaic language, which has largely departed from a uniform pattern of terse prohibitions like those still preserved in VI-IX.

(iii) G.E. Mendenhall's argument has already been alluded to in Chapter 2.V and need be only briefly recapitulated here. He uses an essentially form-critical argument to push the potential origin of the Decalogue back to the Mosaic period. He points out that apodeictic law was not peculiar to ancient Israel: it was to be found in the LBA Hittite Vassal Treaty. Since this form of treaty was known in the Mediterranean coastal regions in the later second millennium BC, Israel could have adopted this form to express its covenant with the LORD in that period. Shechem, with the Hittite associations of its indigenous population, the Bene Hamor (Gen. 33.18-34.31), and its tradition of covenant at the shrine of Baal-berith ('the lord of the covenant', Jud. 9.1-57), would have been a suitable place where Israel could have learned the pattern.

(iv) E. Gerstenberger, *Wesen und Herkunft des 'apodiktischen Rechts'* [The Nature and Origin of 'Apodeictic Law'], WMANT 20, Neukirchen, 1965: Alt's form-critical discussion of the Decalogue, in particular, the category of 'apodeictic law' and the *Sitz im Leben* to which he assigned it, is the focus of attention.

Gerstenberger is sceptical of Alt's definition of the Decalogue as 'apodeictic law': only clauses which specify penalty as well as crime can properly be called 'law' and this is clearly not the case with the Ten Words. Most of them should, rather, be termed 'prohibitions'.

He also rejects Alt's ritual of covenant-making or renewal as the *Sitz im Leben* of the Decalogue. The terms of a covenant should relate to the relationship between the two covenant partners. But in the Decalogue only I and II, which expressly safeguard the exclusiveness of the relationship, would fit as the stipulations of a covenant between Yahweh and Israel. While the home of these stipulations in the cult might even be conceded, most of the other prohibitions (and commandments), especially V-X, are concerned with the individual's social responsibilities. Their presence in a liturgy of covenant-renewal can at best be secondary.

What, then, is the primary setting of the prohibition? The prohibition 'don't do. . . ' is an elemental and universal feature in human speech, particularly related to the bringing-up of children within the family. That might seem at first sight to be a truism of little value for further elucidation of the question. But the chief example which Gerstenberger finds in the Old Testament carries some conviction, viz. Jer. 35.6ff., the commandments which Jonadab son of Rechab imposed as 'father' on his 'family' and which they then observed for at least two hundred years. The prohibition is expressed in 2nd person imperfect + the negative *lo'*, 'not', as in the Decalogue. The verb in Jeremiah is in the plural as opposed to the singular of the Decalogue, because the members are being thought of collectively; the singular would be equally apposite for the individual. The commandments of Jonadab are termed *d^ebarim*, 'words' (v. 14), precisely the term for the clauses of the Decalogue in, e.g., Exod. 20.1. The individual prohibition appears not in isolation but in a series, in this case of four (cf. the series of ten, or possibly sub-series of four and six, in the Decalogue; shorter series are in any case much more typical of the genre); there are also positive commandments with result clause (v. 7, cf. V). The reference of such prohibitions/ commandments is to the preservation of family life (cf. V-X). They can thus be related to other such lists, e.g. Lev. 18.7ff., which are concerned with safeguarding the integrity of the family. The prohibition is comparable to the instruction of Wisdom Literature, both Israelite (e.g. Prov. 1-9; 22.17ff.) and international, and it is within the context of the wise that its *Sitz im Leben* is to be placed. The chief exponents of the genre would then be the head of the household, the hierarchy of brothers and sons within the extended family and the elders within the community. The authority of the father arose not simply because of his position in the family but because of the sacral order of life which he represented. In the course of time, aspects of this clan instruction were developed and taken over by both the professional priest and the wise man and combined with other materials in cult, law and wisdom. This would suggest that the emergence of the Decalogue as a collection was later rather than earlier.

3. *Canonical criticism*

For the sake of the completeness of the illustration of the issues by means of the Decalogue, brief allusion may be made to Childs' typically perceptive comment on the function of the Decalogue in the 'canonical form' of the Exodus text. The Decalogue occupies a key position: the prologue, Exod. 20.2, summarizes the preceding chapters, Exodus 1–18; the 'ten commandments' in Exod. 20.3-17 provide the authoritative guide to all the succeeding legal material (*Introduction*, 174).

4. *The literary approach*

Equally briefly—for here, above all, the response of the individual interpreter is in play—possibilities for a literary interpretation may be noted. The unevenness in length of the individual 'commandments' is not to be regarded as an anomaly to be corrected by the imposition of a uniform pattern suggested by literary or form criticism. Disparity is of significance in itself. For example, it throws the sabbath commandment, IV, as the most elaborated, firmly into the centre of attention; duties to God and to man are then roughly symmetrically disposed on either side of it; the two positive commands, IV and V, which elicit active implementation, as opposed to the negative commands which merely require avoidance, are placed side by side.

5. *Redaction criticism*

Redaction criticism is concerned with the process of the growing together of the elements which gradually produces the whole; 'redaction' strongly implies the final stages of editing *written* materials and 'redaction criticism' an interest in editorial intention and the function of a passage within its literary context, whatever prehistory it may have passed through in whole or in part.

Illuminating and legitimate though literary critical and form critical discussions may be, it must be abundantly clear that there is a strong element of the hypothetical within the reconstructions of the earlier phases reviewed in Chapter 3.VI.1 and 2. It is certainly more secure to ask redactio-historically about the function of the Decalogue in the virtually assured various stages of the evolution of the literary text, for which I have argued in Chapter 3.IV. The more modest redactio-historical aim of doing justice to the intention of the editors of the two levels of the D-version and the P-edition is more certainly attainable, and ensures that an appropriate degree of dialectic between canonical varieties of theology (the redemption of the first-born, covenant and eschatology of the D-version and the presence of God, holiness and realized eschatology in the P-edition, as will be argued in Chapter 4.II and III) is preserved in the interpretation of the text.

There is no reason to doubt that the D-version of Exodus included the Decalogue at precisely its present location (contra the views of F.-L. Hossfeld): the parallels on the giving of the Decalogue in Deut. 4.10-15; 5, on which the argument in Chapter 3.IV.3, has largely depended, indicate that this is so. The version of the Decalogue in Deut. 5.6-21, shorn of its features as 'retrospect' (especially the recurring phrase, 'as the LORD your God commanded you', e.g. Deut. 5.12), is likely to give good evidence for the D-version of the Decalogue which once stood in Exod. 20.2-17 before the final redaction of the P-edition. The major contribution of the P-edition's revision of the D-version of the Decalogue is the motive for keeping the sabbath in IV.

The D-version of Exodus provides the exilic account of Israel's origins. In its present context in the D-version the Decalogue ceases to be (if it ever was) a reflection of particular historical and social conditions as at the end of the eighth century (as on the interpretation of F. Crüsemann). Rather, the Decalogue can now be seen as an ideal, eschatological, statement—however much it utilizes the social and historical data of the past—looking towards the future realization of Israel's life of freedom under the LORD. It is within this perspective that some of the puzzling omissions of the Decalogue, e.g. the lack of reference to the care of the widow and the orphan and to the other social concerns of the prophets, can be understood. For all Israel in that eschaton will realize the perfect plan of the settlement whereby every family, including its weakest members, each settled inviolably on its own farmland, will have provision made for its support. Within that context full humanitarian consideration can be given to the slave (whether voluntary [Deut. 15.16f.] or foreign prisoner of war). The Decalogue in the D-version is, thus, a document full of theological pathos: the people of the LORD presently 'enslaved' in exile or diaspora, lacking land, the basic condition of the freedom which is God's gift, suffering perhaps even the loss of their former lands, properties and wives, not just at the hands of their enemies but even of their rapacious former neighbours who have been spared the catastrophe (cf. Ezek. 11.14-21; 33.23-29), reaffirm their faith in their God as redeemer, who, as once from Egypt so again from Exile, will one day restore them to an ideal state of liberty.

In the final P-edition of Exodus, no doubt to be dated in the post-exilic period of the 'return', the Decalogue becomes a document of 'realized eschatology'. The 'return from exile' may have been accomplished, but only to a partial degree. The definitive 'Return' is still outstanding. The function of the Decalogue in the P-edition is thus to portray how to live in the eschaton of an ideal that is not yet historically fulfilled; how to make that eschaton 'proleptically present' in the time of waiting for the consummation; how to create the 'enabling environment' within which the realization of that day can be accomplished.

The differences of emphasis of D-version and P-edition focus conveniently on the sabbath. For D (Deut 5.15) it is for exiles a poignant reminder of freedom from slavery and its observance provides a proleptic experience of eschatological return to the freedom of the promised land. For P it is to participate in the ideal equilibrium of creation (Exod. 20.11; cf. Gen. 2.1-3), the rest of the perfection of creation on the seventh day, which provides a proleptic experience of the eschatological Jubilee, when conditions in the land will return to their pristine ideal.

The overtly theological character of these observations on the purpose of the D-version and of the P-edition of the Decalogue lead appropriately into the final chapter.

Further Reading

A review of Decalogue research up to the mid-1960s is to be found in

J.J. Stamm, M.E. Andrew, *The Ten Commandments in Recent Research*, Studies in Biblical Theology, Second Series, 2, London: SCM, 1967.

I have given some account of two important recent studies:

F. -L. Hossfeld, *Der Dekalog: Seine späten Fassungen, die originale Komposition und seine Vorstufen*, OBO 45, Freiburg: Universitätsverlag Göttingen: Vandenhoeck & Ruprecht, 1982.

F. Crüsemann, *Bewahrung der Freiheit: Das Thema des Dekalogs in sozial-geschichtlicher Perspektive*, Kaiser Traktate 78, Munich, 1983, in 'The Decalogue and the Redaction of the Sinai Pericope in Exodus', *ZAW* 100, 1988, 361ff., and 'The "Ten Commandments": some recent interpretations', *ET* 100, 1988-89, 453ff.

A.T.S. Library
Nyack, NY 10960   22175

4

MATTERS THEOLOGICAL:
THE PERVASIVE INTENTION

THIS FINAL CHAPTER assumes that the argument just presented about the literary formation of Exodus is tolerably sound. One may be rather sceptical about the possibility of tracing back by means of the analysis of *this* narrative the course of the evolution of the various materials which go to make up the book. Little time will be spent on inquiry into the theology of such hypothetical earlier stages. Out of the vast reservoir of traditions, the writers have produced in two main phases, the exilic D-version and the restoration P-edition, a verisimilitude of life at the time of Israel's origin. The purpose has not been to recreate the historical events in themselves so much as to illuminate the experience of their contemporaries and of succeeding generations.

I. The revelation of the divine name 'Yahweh'

For the Hebrews a name could be held to express the nature of the person who bore that name (cf. 1 Sam. 25.25). The meaning of the name of God, with which the Decalogue itself opens, may thus be of fundamental importance for Israel's theology. Significantly, both the D-version and the P-edition base their presentations on the revelation of the divine name (Exod. 3.13ff. for D; 6.2ff. for P).

1. *The form of the divine name: 'Yahweh', not 'Jehovah'*
The pronunciation of the proper name of God, except once annually by the High Priest on the Day of Atonement, was forbidden in Judaism. The prohibition was justified exegetically by appeal to Lev. 24.16, where the verb *naqab*, rendered 'blaspheme' in RSV, was understood in the sense of 'pronounce distinctly' (as in its occurrence

in Isa. 62.2). Where the divine name, YHWH, stands in the written text of the Old Testament, the practice was to *read* instead "᾿Adonay', 'my Lord'. The traditional consonants, YHWH, naturally could not be removed from the written text but, to mark the change of reading, they were provided with vowels equivalent to those in "᾿Adonay'. (The difference in the first vowel of the resulting combination, Y᷄HoWaH, is explained by the fact that in Hebrew it is 'indistinct', pronounced as an 'a' with the glottal stop with which "᾿Adonay' begins, but as an 'e' with the Y of YHWH.) The reading of the non-form 'Jehovah' is ascribed to Petrus Galatinus (AD 1460-1540), father-confessor of Pope Leo X.

Evidence of the vowels original to YHWH comes from early Christian sources: e.g. Clement of Alexandria (AD 150-215) 'Iaoue'; Epiphanius (AD 315-403), Theodoret (AD 393-466) 'Iabe'. These Greek forms suggest that the vowels in the first and second syllables of YHWH were *a* and *e*, respectively, hence 'YaHWeH' (the variations in the consonants arise from the fact that the Attic/Koine Greek alphabet has neither *Y, H* nor *W*!). The probability of the resultant reading of the name as 'Yahweh' is confirmed by its being a recognizable Hebrew form—a third person singular masculine imperfect verb—and this is how the Old Testament itself, especially Exod. 3.14f., certainly also understands it.

2. *The meaning of the name Yahweh*
The name 'Yahweh' occurs some 6,823 times in the Old Testament and is attested outside the Old Testament, e.g. in the Mesha‘ Stele (ca. 840), at Kuntillat Ajrud (9th-8th century) and in the Arad and Lachish ostraca (6th century).

Though the name is recognizable as a verbal form (and even that is not universally agreed), there is multiple ambiguity about every other feature—stem, conjugation, person, tense and the identity of its subject and predicate. This ambiguity is compounded by the addition of the relative clause ('. . . WHO I AM') in Exod. 3.14. It may be that this ambiguity is fundamental to the revelation of the Name: Yahweh has made himself known by his name; he can be known as he makes himself known and rational statements can be made about that knowledge; he can be invoked by name. Yet he can never be completely known as he is in himself or as he may be in his actions. This paradox of veiled mystery yet of knowledge revealed to his people is well expressed in Deut. 29.29[Heb.28]. Some of the elements of the ambiguity will be explored below.

(i) Stem: Assuming the name to be a verbal form, there are four possible stems with which it could be associated: HW 'fall' (of snow; Job 37.6); HWH 'desire' (cf. Mic. 7.3; Prov. 10.3, etc.); HWH 'become', rare synonym (Aramaic?) of the fourth possibility, the common Hebrew verb HYH 'be'.

While appropriate senses have been suggested for a name derived from the first two roots—Yahweh as originally a weather God, cf. Baal; Yahweh as passionate, 'jealous'—Exod. 3.14 interprets YHWH in accordance with the last. This may be a popular, rather than a scientifically accurate, etymology, giving the Israelite stamp of understanding to an inherited term.

On the basis of biblical material itself the hypothesis has been put forward that the name 'Yahweh' was of Kenite origin. Certainly it was in the service of his father-in-law, Jethro, priest of Midian, that Moses first encountered Yahweh at the mountain of God (Exodus 3). In Exodus 18 Jethro takes the lead in sacrifice and in the communion meal; he offers Moses counsel about the discharge of justice within the community. Jethro is also called a Kenite (Judg. 1.16) and subsequent Kenites in the Old Testament are notable for their Yahwistic zeal (Judg. 4.11, 17ff.; 2 Kgs 10.15ff., cf. 1 Chron. 2.55). B. Rothenberg has discovered a Midianite tent-shrine complete with brazen serpent (cf. Num. 21.8). The tradition of the knowledge of Yahweh since the generation of Cain, the eponymous ancestor of the Kenites (Gen. 4.26), in contrast to the traditions that the name was first revealed to Moses (Exod. 3; 6), may then have historical foundation.

On the significance of a possible non-Israelite origin of the name Yahweh, S.R. Driver has already said all that is necessary (*Exodus*, li): 'The *source* from which either this or any other divine name was ultimately derived by the Hebrews, matters little or nothing: the question which is of importance is, What did the name *come to mean* to them?. . . We can await with perfect calmness whatever the future may have to disclose to us with regard to its ultimate origin, or its pre-Israelite use'.

(ii) Conjugation: If the name is a 3rd s.m. imperfect verb with the prefix ya-, the conjugation should be causative (*hiph'il*; the intransitive conjugation, *qal*, has the prefix yi-). In that case the name describes the activity of a creator god, who brings into being. But, on the other hand, Exod. 3.14, in providing the 1st s.c. imperfect prefix 'e-, interprets the name as derived from the intransitive stem of the verb (*qal*; the causative conjugation, *hiph'il*, would have the prefix 'a-).

The explanation in Exod. 3.14 thus understands the name in terms of 'being', not of 'creating'.

(iii) Person: In form, Yahweh is 3rd person s.m., 'he. . . '. However, Exod. 3.14 interprets as 1st person s.c., 'I. . . '. In thus emphasizing the first person, it is comparable to the 'divine self-predication' formula 'I am . . . ', especially in the 'prologue' to the Decalogue (cf. the first part of the 'covenant formula', 'I will be your God. . . ', e.g. in Exod. 6.7). In the explanation of Exod. 3.14, Yahweh is not an objective, indirectly referred to 'he', but the personal, relational subject 'I', who is not merely addressed as 'Thou' but who takes the initiative of addressing as 'I'.

(iv) Tense: Traditionally, the name is regarded as a verb in the present tense, 'he is'. Cf. the LXX of Exod. 3.14, 'I am the one who is'; Vulgate, 'I am who I am'; hence EVV, 'I am'. If so, the statement is primarily ontological concerning the eternity of the being of God.

Nonetheless, the verb is more naturally taken in Hebrew in the future tense, 'he will be'. If so, the statement is primarily soteriological, a promise of continuing activity, even an eschatological affirmation.

(v) The openness of subject and predicate: The personal pronoun subject, 'I'/'he', and, thus, the deity who bears the name Yahweh, awaits identification. Hence, already in the Old Testament, there are the possibilities of the equation of Yahweh with the patriarchal God of the father (Exod. 3.13ff.) and with El (Exod. 6.3), no doubt the supreme deity of the north-west Semitic pantheon (cf. Abraham's encounter with El-Shaddai at Hebron[?] in Gen. 17.1, and Jacob's at Bethel in Gen. 35.11).

Equally, the complement of the verb 'to be' needs to be supplied ('I am/he is. . . '). The name must be concretized through experience (e.g. deliverance from Egypt; gift of land) and is open to new experience in which the former is renewed and revitalized.

(vi) The force of the relative clause in Exod. 3.14, '. . . who I am/will be': Some argue, on the basis of the syntax of the Hebrew relative clause (cf. GK 138.d), that the translation should be 'I am the one who is'.

Exod. 3.14 is often elucidated on the basis of Exod. 33.19, where again relative clauses pose a similar syntactical problem: 'I will be gracious to whom I will be gracious; I will have compassion on whom I will have compassion'. Some take this as a paronomasia used to express totality and intensity, 'I am truly the one to have compassion and show pity'. Others object that such paronomasia expresses not totality but vagueness. Therefore, Exod. 3.14 ('I am/shall be who/ what I am') is to be regarded as a revelation which is also a concealment, a statement of God's being or action which veils the fulness of that being or action, and safeguards the transcendence, otherness and freedom of God (cf. Gen. 32.29, Judg. 13.18). Herein lies the theological basis for the ineffability of the divine name in Jewish tradition (cf. *b.Pes.* 50a on Exod. 3.15 which reads not 'this is my name for ever [*leʿolam*]', but the same consonantal text with different vowels, 'this is my name to be concealed [*leʿallem*]').

Further Reading

F.M. Cross, 'Yahweh and the God of the Patriarchs', *HTR* 55, 1962, 225ff.

B. Albrektson, 'On the Syntax of *'ehyeh ªsher 'ehyeh* in Exodus 3.14', in P.R. Ackroyd, B. Lindars, eds., *Words and Meanings: Essays presented to David Winton Thomas*, Cambridge University Press, 1968, 15ff.

M. Rose, *Jahwe: Zum Streit um den alttestamentlichen Gottesnamen*, Zürich: Theologischer Verlag, 1978.

Etymology marks only one stage, and particularly in this case not the most eloquent one, in the elucidation of meaning. The Old Testament as a whole, not least the rest of the book of Exodus, is the exposition of the character of YHWH, the deity who bears that name. In conformity with the redactio-historical argument pursued above, the nature of the deity who bears the name Yahweh may be expounded first in the terms of the D-version and then of the P-edition.

II. The theology of the D-version

The complementarity of the D-version and the P-edition noted at the end of Chapter 3.VI.5 in connection with the Decalogue, can be extended in a number of respects: the relative roles of Moses and Aaron, the religious institutions through which Israel focused their relationship with Yahweh (Firstlings—as well as Passover—and covenant in D; Passover—as well as Unleavened Bread—and sanctuary in P) and the theological statement implied by these institutions (justification in D; sanctification in P), with their associated eschatologies.

1. *Moses*

The heart of the D-version, in the parts of Exod. 19.3-20.21
attributable to it, concerns revelation, God's initiative of self-
disclosure. Revelation occurs both in theophany, which inspires awe
and the subjugation of the will, and in rational communication,
expressed in instruction and personal guidance.

The whole people gathered at the foot of Mt Horeb share directly
in overwhelming experiences of vision and audition. The narrative
describes the essentially immediate nature of the relationship
between Yahweh and people in terms of an original moment of
preparation for covenant; at this moment of fundamental significance,
Moses functions merely as marshal. The people see for themselves
the terrifying appearing of God above them on the mountain-top.
That terror is increased by the impenetrability of the storm-cloud by
which the mystery of God is veiled: the appearance of God as he is in
himself is beyond human capacity to conceive or endure. This vision
is accompanied by a no less overwhelming experience of hearing, the
crash of the thunder-roll and the trumpet alarms of cosmic battle.
The purpose of this vision and audition is to catch the people up
directly into the unforgettable experience of an immediate encounter
with God, to the utter limit that such an encounter is conceivable
and endurable for ordinary humanity. This once-for-all experience of
overwhelming direct personal encounter with their own very God,
who has just rescued them from slavery and danger and brought
them to freedom, is to be the basis and reference-point of their
continuing life. Constantly recalled and realized in its inexpungeable
memory, it is to become the fundamental assumption and constitute
the essential fabric of personal and corporate identity. The 'fear of
Yahweh' is the basic posture expected of the people from now on
(Exod. 20.20).

Even here, the immediate personal experience of being utterly
overwhelmed by encounter with the impenetrable mystery and
unimaginable majesty of God is accompanied by rational communication: the 'Ten Words', God's own very speech, heard directly,
unmediated, by their own very ears. In the Decalogue the fundamental
principles of God's continuing relationship with his people, and their
social relationship therein with one another, are expressed in
unambiguous and unqualified terms. Easily memorised in their
clarity, conciseness and accessibility they are intended to be as
unforgettable as the awesome experience of the encounter itself.

It is only in the service of this primary experience of the people's direct, unmediated, encounter with its God that Moses assumes his role. His role is that of supreme prophet: he is spokesman and agent for God, intermediary between God and people, mediator of covenant and intercessor for the people, even ready to offer himself vicariously on their behalf. The portrayal of Moses as prophet matches the definition of his status as prophet in Deuteronomy (see, especially, Deut. 5.23-26; 13.1-5; 18.15-22; 34.10-12). There are also close parallels to be drawn between Moses and other prophets in the Dtr corpus, especially Elijah, the first of the great reforming prophets of the northern monarchy (cf. the parallel experiences of theophany in Exodus 33 and 1 Kgs. 19), and Jeremiah, the last of the reform prophets who lived through the terminal decline and final collapse of the southern monarchy (cf. the call narratives in Exodus 3f. and Jeremiah 1—probably elaborated by the Dtr editors—with the motifs of the sign of the burning bush/almond tree and of the youth and inarticulateness of the two figures).

As Yahweh's agent, Moses receives his credentials ('how will they believe in me?') in the power to work signs (Exod. 4.1-9). His shepherd's staff becomes a wonder-working rod; by it he effects the plagues which are in principle the handiwork of Yahweh (e.g. Exod. 4.17; 9.23; 10.13). Their purpose is so to heighten the obduracy of Pharaoh that the manifestation of Yahweh's power and glory may be the greater (cf. Exod. 14.17). Moses' rod is instrumental again for the revelation of Yahweh's power through Moses at the Red Sea (Exod. 14.16, 21, 31 ['and they believed in Yahweh and his servant Moses']) and in the incidents of water from the rock (Exod. 17.5 referring back to the first plague, Exod. 7.17) and of deliverance from the Amalekites (Exod. 17.8ff.).

Moses' intimacy with Yahweh is indicated by his encounter at the mountain of God, Horeb, (Exod. 3.1–4.17; 18.1-12) and by his lone converse (e.g. Exod. 19.3-9, 19; 24.12, 18; 31.18–32.20; 32.30–33.6; 34.1, 4-28) and unparalleled vision on the mountain-top (Exod. 33.12-23). Herein Moses receives his credentials as recipient of revelation (Exod. 19.9, 'that they may believe in you'). After Horeb, this intimacy continues at the tent of meeting (Exod. 33.7-11): revelation remains in the form of rationally accessible guidance through the mediator to the people.

Moses' role as mediator of the covenant is dramatically presented by his continual reporting of the speech of each side to the other (Exod. 19.3-9), by his writing the terms of the covenant in the Book of the Covenant and organization of the covenant rite (Exod. 24.3-8) and by his reception of the tablets of the Decalogue engraved by the finger of Yahweh (Exod. 24.12, 18; 31.18). His mediatorial role rises to its greatest intensity in the aftermath of the golden calf incident in his intercession and offering of himself for vicarious punishment (Exod. 32.30-33) and reaches its conclusion in the mediation of the covenant remade on the original terms (Exod. 34.1, 4-28).

2. The Dtrc. exposition of the Name of Yahweh in terms of exodus, covenant and renewal of the covenant

(i) *Exodus*: The D-version of the narrative of the exodus in Exod. 1.1-15.21 follows the sequence of Deut. 15.12–16.8, i.e. the D legislation on the freeing of the Hebrew slave (Deut. 15.12-18), the dedication of the first-born (Deut. 15.19-23) and the observation of the passover (Deut. 16.1-8). It is the exposition in narrative form of this legislation. It opens with the resounding statement in Exod. 4.22f., which combines the themes of the three sets of legislation, 'Say to Pharaoh, "Thus says Yahweh, 'Israel is my first-born son. . . Let my son go that he may serve me. If you refuse to let him go, behold, I will slay your first-born son.'"' This combination of the motifs 'first-born', 'setting the slave free' and 'to serve', i.e., 'be slaves' to Yahweh sets the theme of the D-version of the exodus.

The institutional focus of the Dtrc. exodus narrative is *not* the Passover as such but the offering of the first-born (cf. Chapter 3.IV.3(iv) (b)) (as, indeed, the connecting of these institutions in the narrative with the climactic tenth plague—the death of the Egyptian first-born—would lead us to expect). Israel is Yahweh's first-born, who at the cost of Egypt's first-born owes life, freedom and prosperity to Yahweh; in turn, they owe all their first-born to Yahweh as an expression of gratitude. Thus the slaying of the first-born of Egypt, both of man and of beast, leads directly to the legislation on Israel's offering of the first-born of their animals and the redemption of the first-born of their sons (Exod. 13.1-16). Because of the centralization of the cult in D, the offering of the first-born of animals no longer takes place locally on the eighth day (as in the earlier legislation of the Book of the Covenant, Exod. 22.29f. [Heb. 28f.]) but centrally and annually (Deut. 15.20) in connection with the festival of Unleavened Bread interpreted as Passover (Deut. 15.12–16.8). The commemoration of the exodus is thus two-fold: annually at the festival of Unleavened Bread/Passover, and also perennially in the visible preservation of the first-born male of every family. Hence in Exodus 13, while unleavened bread is indeed to be eaten annually in the month of Abib in commemoration of the exodus (vv. 3-10), it is subordinated to the perpetual recollection of Israel's redemption at the cost of the first-born by being enclosed within legislation for the offering of the first-born (vv. 1-2, 11-16).

It is perhaps within this context that the deeply enigmatic section Exod. 4.24-26, Yahweh's attempt on Moses' life, may be understood. It is fitting that Moses, the leader of Israel, redeemed at the cost of the Egyptian first-born and consecrated by the dedication of their own first-born, should himself be redeemed by the blood of the circumcision, the symbol of the dedication to Yahweh, of his own first-born son.

(ii) *Covenant*: In the D-version, the narrative passes directly from the crossing of the Red Sea to Horeb, i.e. from deliverance to covenant. The 'prologue' to the Decalogue in Exod. 20.2, 'I am Yahweh, your God, who has brought you out of the land of Egypt, out of the house of slaves', succinctly states the essence of the matter. Everything depends on the nature and action of the God who reveals himself by the name 'Yahweh'. Israel find themselves in relationship with Yahweh not by choice on their part but thanks alone to his initiative. It is in this relationship that they are brought into being and into full status as a free people.

The formalization of this relationship in covenant now follows. It is the central contribution of the theologians of the D/Dtr school to have explored the concept 'covenant'. 'Covenant' is undoubtedly a term borrowed from everyday social and economic life for agreements which contain contractual obligations (cf. Chapter 2.V). But when this concept is turned from the 'horizontal' (inter-human) plane to the 'vertical' (the relation between Yahweh and Israel) the term has to undergo theological modification. How can Yahweh, inscrutable in his transcendence and sovereign in his autonomy, be bound as covenant partner? How can the people of Israel as human beings ever do anything for God, since all that they are and have they have received from him in the first place? If Israel cannot do anything for God in its obedience, how much less in its disobedience! However solemn the covenant and sincere the commitment to it at the moment of its original conclusion, however awesome the theophany of Yahweh, which accompanies it, however absolutely binding its terms, Israel falls away in the emblematic sin of the golden calf (Exodus 32).

The Dtr theologians write in the context of exile, where they reflect on the mystery of Israel's preservation in the midst of the exile, understood as punishment for sins committed ever since Horeb. Israel is Yahweh's first-born son, but in its long history it has proved itself rebellious. By law the refractory son should be put to death (cf. Deut. 21.18-21). How is it, then, that Israel has not utterly perished? The answer can only lie in the forgiving mercy and long-suffering grace of Yahweh himself. It is for this reason, therefore, that the Dtr theologians have reformulated the law-code of Exod. 20.22–23.19 as a covenant-code and called it the 'Book of the Covenant' (cf. Chapter 3.IV.3(ii)): the law-code with its penalties is now enfolded in the covenant-code; the penalty for breach of covenant-code now depends on the autonomous will of the divine covenant partner, 'who will be gracious to whom he will be gracious' (Exod. 33.19). The conventional term 'justification' (even without faith in the recipient!) can, with full appropriateness, be used of Dtrc. theology.

(iii) *Eschatology*: But the terms of the covenant unilaterally abrogated by Israel remain valid. Therefore, the covenant is remade in Exodus 34 on the identical terms of Decalogue and B, as before (cf. Chapter 3.IV.3(iii) (c)). But the Dtr. theologians are aware that only if Yahweh himself in the end provides the conditions whereby Israel can be faithful to its terms can the covenant ever be maintained by them. Beyond the confines of Exodus, the D/Dtr school look forward to the day when God will inscribe the terms of the covenant, not on stone tablets but on the fleshy tablets of the heart of each member of the community, so that all God's people with immediate knowledge of his commandments will be enabled to keep the covenant (cf. Deut. 30.1-10; Jer. 31.31-34).

III. The theology of the P-edition

The P-edition of Exodus contributes especially the material on genealogies in chapters 1 and 6; itineraries in chapters 12–19; the emphasis on Aaron in chapters 6–11 and in subsequent chapters; the Passover in chapter 12 and sabbath in chapter 16, ritual purity and hierarchy in chapters 19, 24, 34 and the tabernacle in chapters 25–31.17; 35–40, along with a host of more detailed adjustments of the underlying D-version. Since this later edition of Exodus belongs to the final promulgation of the whole Pentateuch as scripture in the post-exilic period, it ought properly to be viewed as part of the overall statement of the final editors within the comprehensive chrono-logical and genealogical schemata they provide for the Pentateuch, as well as within the rather narrower frameworks of the wilderness itineraries (cf. Numbers 33) and of the large central block on 'revelation at Sinai' (Exod. 19.1–Num. 10.10). That can be done to only a marginal extent in this context. Put very generally and partially, the P-edition of the Pentateuch is concerned with the forms, projected into an idealized primal time for purposes of sanction, which continuing life under God should take in the period of 'realized eschatology' between the 'return from exile', which turned out to be limited in both scale and quality, and the definitive 'Return' which Israel awaits in the final Jubilee.

For the P-edition, the revelation of the divine name 'Yahweh', deliverance from slavery and the covenantal relationship are as primary (Exod. 6.2-9) as for the D-version. The P-edition of Exodus, however, complements the D-version with a number of important contributions.

1. *The status of Aaron*

The P-writer is naturally concerned with Aaron as the 'father' of the Aaronic priesthood of the Second Temple. He is as aware as the D-version that Aaron remains subordinate to Moses: the sacrificial cult, which can be observed in the name of any god (cf. the golden calf incident and Israel's Canaanite background), is ambiguous in itself and is only acceptable if given the normative interpretation of Yahwism, which stems from the revelation to Moses (cf. P's addition in Exod. 34.29-35 on the radiance of the face of Moses after he has communed with Yahweh). The Aaronic priesthood as officiants in the cult can then only operate within the more general 'Levitical' framework of the teaching of Moses, the Levite. This is put genealogically in terms of the fact that the family of Aaron is only one branch within the tribe of Levi (Exod. 6.16-25); it is expressed in narrative form in the bloody ordination of the Levites as Yahweh zealots in Exod. 32.20b-29. The roles of the Levites are wider than cultic matters, concerning primarily instruction and the monitoring of Israel's obedience to the precepts of the law (cf. Deut. 33.8-11).

Central to P's conception of the maintenance of the bond between Yahweh and Israel are the sacrificial rites practised at the altar by the Aaronic priests. By the rites of the Day of Atonement, sanctuary and people are annually sanctified; thereafter, the stated round of sacrifice, whole burnt-offering, communion sacrifice, sin and guilt offering—offered daily, weekly, monthly and at festivals—and the numberless *ad hoc* sacrifices of vow and thanksgiving, by which the restored bond between Yahweh and people is sacramentaly expressed

and maintained, can recommence (cf. e.g. Lev. 16; Num. 28; 29).
Equally significant for the maintenance of good order within the
community is the priestly discrimination of 'the holy and the
common, the clean and the unclean' (Lev. 10.10). Thus in the P-
edition of Exodus the immediacy of Aaron's activity as Moses' agent
in matters of speech and miracle-working (e.g. Exod. 6.27–7.13) and
his close proximity to Moses in the hierarchy on the mountain of
God (e.g. Exod. 19.24) are stressed. The appropriate rites for the
ordination of the Aaronic priesthood and the specification of their
vestments are duly given in Exod. 28; 29; 30.30 (cf. 39; Lev. 8.1-
36).

2. *Realized eschatology*
In the Pentateuch the D-version of the journey through the
wilderness is the dynamic, eschatological one of progression, from
deliverance to covenant to emblematic rebellion, and then from
covenant remade through repeated rebellions to covenant renewed
on the plains of Moab, so that Israel stands poised on the verge of
entry into the land. The P-edition's account is the static one of the
prevailing situation of human rebellion, despite the revelation of
divine ordinances at the heart of life. In the time of waiting between
the return from exile and the last Jubilee, Israel is in a constant
condition of recalcitrant 'murmuring' against Yahweh, though he has
done everything by the revelation of ordinance and institution, to
enable that condition of holiness by which his people can proleptically
anticipate the end-time. Thus for the P-writer the Sinai pericope,
Exod. 19.1–Num. 10.10, stands centrally, with the incidents of the
murmuring of the people and the answering provision by Yahweh,
repeatedly and unwearyingly granted, disposed somewhat symmetrically on either side (cf. Chapter 3.IV.3(iv)(a)).

It may thus be fairly claimed that whereas the D-version is about
justification—the ever-renewed restoration of the rebellious people
in the long-suffering grace of Yahweh till they stand poised on the
verge of their inheritance—the P-edition is about sanctification, the
possibilities of holy living now, even in the long in-between time of
waiting for the final consummation.

3. *Institutional focus*
As befits priestly preoccupation, the regulations for the domestic
rites of Passover and the Temple rites of Unleavened Bread,
combined in such unprecedented manner in Deut. 16.1-8 (cf. 2 Kgs

23.21-23 and Exod. 13.3-10), are carefully distinguished (Exod. 12.1-28, 43-50).

In accord with the theme of sanctification the P-writer in the context of covenant-making at Sinai in Exod. 19-24 stresses ritual purity for the encounter with Yahweh and strict hierarchy in those who dare venture towards his presence. Thus Moses, the recipient of direct revelation, stands at the apex of Mount Sinai; while Aaron and his sons and seventy elders share the covenant meal on the mountain, the young men and people share in the covenant rite on the plain below (Exod. 24.1-2, 5, 6, 8, 9-11).

Equally, the detailed specification of the tabernacle and its furnishings and equipment (Exod. 25.1-27.21; 30.1-31.11) and the meticulous execution of that specification in Exod. 35.1-38.31; 39.32-40.33 express the concept of the holy in spatial and material terms. But the mere external form, even when elaborated to this astonishing degree, is not the fundamental matter. The pervading purpose is that the external physical environment may be created wherein Yahweh, at his own behest, may fittingly bestow his presence. Exod. 40.34-38 thus forms the appropriate climax of the work: when all has been prepared by the action and revelation of Yahweh himself, his own presence is granted to his people for constant hallowing and guidance.

Further Reading

There are numerous *theologies* of the Old Testament available in English, e.g. L. Koehler (1957), E. Jacob (1958), T.C. Vriezen (1958), G.A.F. Knight (1959), W. Eichrodt (I, 1961; II, 1967), G. von Rad (I, 1962; II, 1965), J.L. McKenzie (1974), W. Zimmerli (1978), R.E. Clements (1978), C. Westermann (1982), W.H. Schmidt (1983), B.S. Childs (1985).

For the Deuteronomic movement in general, cf.

M. Weinfeld, *Deuteronomy and the Deuteronomic School*, Oxford: Clarendon, 1972.

For the theological impact of the Deuteronomic movement on the formation of Israel's literature during the exilic period, cf. e.g.

J. Vermeylen, *Le Dieu de la promesse et le Dieu de l'alliance*, Lectio Divina 126, Paris: Editions du Cerf, 1986.

For the theology of P, see e.g.

R.W. Klein, 'The Message of P', in J. Jeremias, L. Perlitt, eds., *Die*

Botschaft und die Boten: Festschrift für Hans Walter Wolff, Neukirchen: Neukirchener Verlag, 1981, 57ff.

M. Saebø, 'Priestertheologie und Priesterschrift', in *Congress Volume, Vienna*, VTS 32, 1981, 357ff.

For a review of the history of the interpretation of the exodus, including its influence on Liberation Theology, see e.g.

B. Van Iersel, A. Weiler, eds., *The Exodus—a Lasting Paradigm*, Concilium 198, Edinburgh: T. & T. Clark, 1987.

INDEXES

INDEX OF BIBLICAL REFERENCES